BE ORIGIN.

Do you think of yourself as original?

Are you happy to go your own way and do your own thing, even if it's different from what your friends are doing? Perhaps you take pride in your unique sense of style and always voice your own opinion. Or are you usually influenced by others? Do you dress in the same way as your friends and have similar ideas and interests to them?

If it's the latter, you might feel that it's better to fit in than do or say something that will make you stand out. Perhaps you worry that you'd be mocked or left out of the group. But you might also feel this is holding you back and stopping you from expressing your true self.

So, whether you want to delve into your creative side, become more assured in speaking up or simply take some time to consider your goals and dreams, this is the book for you. We hope it inspires you to be bold, show your true colours and express yourself your way.

FIND YOUR CONFIDENCE

CONTENTS

DREAM BIG, BE ASPIRATIONAL

Why it's important to work towards your future goals now

Have you come across the word aspirational? If you're aspirational, it means you have a desire to achieve a high level of success, whether that involves going to university, running your own business, becoming a doctor, writing a book or representing your country at a sport you love. It could be something else entirely – but still a big goal. So, are you aspirational? If not, and you don't have dreams and goals for the future, it's time to change. It might not always feel like it, but school days are among the most exciting times of your life. You might be thinking: 'Exciting, really? Going to class after class? All that homework?' Yes! School years are exciting because at this stage, anything is possible. It's only a short period of your life (really), but it's a springboard to achieving whatever you want to do. Here are some reminders of why you need to make the most of your time as a student and aim for your dream...

REACH FOR THE STARS

Start dreaming

If you could do anything in life, what would it be? Forget about looking silly, or whether people will tell you to be more realistic. It could be that you want to be an astronaut, a singer, an engineer, an architect or even a chocolate taster. If you're at school studying hard, you're in a position to achieve whatever you want. There's a saying: 'Shoot for the Moon – even if you miss, you'll land among the stars.' This means aim high and you might get there, but even if you don't, you'll land near to your dream and you won't have regrets because at least you tried.

Do your research

You might find school boring, but most of your life will be spent working so make sure you put yourself in the best possible position to do a job you love. Think about what you love to do. What are your strengths? Find out what your dream job involves – and the qualifications or experience you'll need to be in a position to do it – and start planning your route to get there. As dull as some lessons seem now, they're all leading towards the grades you need to get. School is a stepping stone.

Get help

If you find you're struggling in any of the subjects that are needed to move you towards your end goal, speak to your teachers and ask for help. They're not just there to moan at you for not listening or doing homework. Along with school counsellors, they can help to guide you and share valuable information. Use them by asking questions – they'll be able to give you book recommendations for extra study and share advice on how to keep progressing. If you find certain lessons boring, resolve to work even harder, listen to your teacher and engage in the lessons as best you can knowing that everything is leading up to you achieving your dream at the end of it.

Be prepared for resistance

There might be people who'll be quick to put you down or tell you your dreams are 'too big' or 'unrealistic'. The really important thing is that you have belief in yourself at the same time as being realistic. Yes, your dreams may be big, and you may not achieve them, but that doesn't mean you have to stop going for them. What would have happened if Steve Jobs, the man who co-founded technology giant Apple, had listened to the people who said he wouldn't be successful with the iPhone? Or if multiple grand-slam champion Serena Williams had given up on her passion to be a tennis player? Believe in yourself and keep pursuing your goals. Remember to 'shoot for the Moon'.

Set small goals

This year, set yourself small goals that you feel will take you a step closer to your dream. It could be achieving a higher grade in a test in a particular subject that's relevant to your goal, never missing a sports practice or gaining some work experience. If you know you have important exams coming up, start attending study sessions or start studying topics you're unsure of from the previous year.

Record your success

Create a diary of all the things you're doing to help you achieve your goal and detail the ups and downs of your journey. When you've achieved your success, you'll be able to look back on how you got there with pride – and one day, perhaps, you'll be that inspirational adult advising teenagers to go for their dreams and to realise that the time to get going on achieving those goals is now.

OH, GO ON THEN!

Say yes to new things and shake up your routine. By pushing past your comfort zone you can open up a world of possibilities

Sometimes it's easier to stick to the things you're comfortable and familiar with and avoid trying new things. After all, what if you fail? Or make a fool of yourself? But there's a lot to be said for saying yes to opportunities. You may learn a new skill, develop a hobby, make friends or even pave the way to an exciting career.

Usually people imagine something to be a lot scarier than it actually is, which makes pushing through your initial fear the hardest part. Have you ever worried about something only to find there was no reason to? Fear of the unknown can prevent you from stepping forward. Often the trickiest part is saying yes in the first place.

There are many ways you can shake up your routine. These can range from gentle changes, such as joining a friend at an after-school class, to big and exciting adventures where you enroll on a course or try a challenging sport. Opening doors to fresh experiences makes life exciting and when you embrace the new, you free your heart and mind, which could potentially lead to somewhere amazing. If you're looking for motivation to try something new, here are a few things to think about...

Be brave
Trying new things increases confidence and builds self-esteem. Saying yes to one opportunity usually motivates you to say yes more often, opening your life to people and adventures. Courage and confidence are wonderful attributes to nurture. They inspire others and make you feel good. Even if you try something and you don't like it, at least you tried. After all, you can take something from everything – even failure.

Live in the here and now
Opening up to challenges and experiences provides a heightened awareness and a greater sense of being present. This means you're less likely to be thinking about the past or worrying about the future. Sometimes all it takes is a small sidestep to break bad habits and see everything more clearly. It's like having a little space to recharge and refocus and, who knows, it may even help you face the more challenging areas of your life.

Make new friends

If you consider where you met your friends it was probably over a shared experience. Seeking out activities is a great way to meet new people, and it's wonderful to learn and share experiences with friends, especially if you can motivate each other along the way.

Be happy

Probably the best thing about trying new things is finding you enjoy them. Life is a joy if you spend it doing the things you love with the people who lift you. So why not seek challenges and seize opportunities when they arise?

Move on

Throughout your life, you may say no to something and later regret your decision. Missing opportunities can feel like you've let yourself down. You may also wish you had more courage and motivation to take yourself forward, especially if you see others thrive on an experience you'd previously declined. Remember it's rarely too late to learn something new and rather than dwelling on a past decision, why not make a promise to say yes the next time an exciting opportunity comes your way?

Who am I?

You learn a lot when you challenge yourself. Trying new things is a good way to better understand who you are and to unlock skills you perhaps didn't know you had. So, whether you've always wanted to try floral styling or harbour a secret desire to skate well, open up to a new experience and realise your full potential.

'ALL THINGS ARE DIFFICULT
BEFORE THEY ARE EASY'

Thomas Fuller

10 NEW THINGS TO TRY TODAY

It's fun to try something different, but it can be easy to fall into the trap of doing the same old things. Need some fresh ideas? Here are 10 new things you could do this weekend, or even today. Why not pick one and see where it takes you?

* Visit somewhere in your town or city you've never been before.
* Volunteer with your local conservation society and help to plant some trees.
* Listen to a genre of music you haven't tried before – blues, reggae, classical?
* Learn 10 phrases in a new language.
* Start writing a diary.
* Try a new food or cuisine – Korean, perhaps, or Polish?
* Plant some flowers in your garden or start an indoor terrarium.
* Say hello to a neighbour you don't usually talk to.
* Go for a bike ride around your neighbourhood.
* Learn how to cook a new dish for dinner.

SHY AND ASPIRING

If you find yourself tongue-tied and red-faced in social situations, you're not alone. Many people are bashful. Being shy is one of the many positive parts that make you who you are and there's no reason it should stop you achieving your dreams

Once you get the first term of a new school year behind you, you may be confidently buzzing with the excitement of having more friends and a calendar bursting with invites. If, however, you're bashful, those first weeks of the new year can be painful. You may have felt tearful or panic-stricken at the thought of walking into a classroom full of unfamiliar faces, blushed or avoided eye contact whenever someone tried to speak to you, and spent break time sitting alone, beating yourself up about not being able to approach people to introduce yourself. You may have been thinking there was something wrong with you.

If that scenario sounds familiar, the first thing to know is that it's simply not true. There's nothing wrong with you. Shyness – broadly defined as feeling anxious around other people, and most intensely so in social situations such as your first day at school – is natural and many people, including those who seem most self-assured, experience it from time to time.

Where does it come from?

Professor Joe Moran, author of *Shrinking Violets: The Secret Life of Shyness*, is an expert on the subject. Deeply shy himself, he says shyness is 'intrinsic' to being a human being.

'Humans are the only self-conscious species – that is, we alone are aware of ourselves and of how we relate and appear to others. To put it simply, what we call "shyness" arises from our desire to be liked.'

Though some people are shyer than others – it's believed to be hereditary – shyness can strike anyone at any time. It also ebbs and flows depending on context and situation, so you might be super chatty and open in one class, yet clam up in another if there are students, or a teacher, who make you feel less comfortable.

Even Kim Kardashian-West – seemingly one of the most attention-seeking celebrities on the planet – admitted she felt shy at times. 'The real Kim is not outspoken and loud like everyone assumes,' she said, 'but actually shy and reserved. I'm the girl who's too nervous to dance in a nightclub.'

Will it affect your goals?

In short, no. Kim's quote reveals it's in no way a barrier to following your dreams and fulfilling your ambitions. Singer Lady Gaga, actors Keira Knightley and Robert Pattinson and writer JK Rowling are among the many successful people who are also bashful. It's something worth bearing in mind the next time you find yourself fretting about walking into a coffee shop on your own or going to a party.

Can shyness be good?

In short, yes. Shyness is one of the (many) characteristics that make you, you, so you should not necessarily seek to change it.

Professor Moran sees it as a personality trait, just like being conscientious or open, and one that has many positives. For example, shy people are often good listeners, more contemplative and empathetic. Their actions and speech are considered, so what they say and do is unlikely to change on a whim, which makes them dependable and constant.

DEALING WITH SHYNESS

While accepting that being shy is part of your nature, finding ways to control it may be helpful. Professor Moran says: 'I fully accept my shyness but felt that having some coping mechanisms would enable me to function more comfortably in social situations.'

Plan ahead
'Shy behaviour can sometimes be misinterpreted as aloofness, which can make forming friendships more difficult initially, so I've moderated how I meet and greet people,' adds Professor Moran. 'I smile, I plan conversations and I carry a notebook with things to say in case I run out of small talk, which helps me feel more secure.'

Ease yourself into uncomfortable situations
Since shyness is really a fear – of drawing attention to or making a fool of yourself, or of being rejected – it might help to confront it. If you can prove to yourself that your fears are unfounded, they'll lose their power over you.

The only way to do this, of course, is to do the things that scare you. Start gently, perhaps by vowing to yourself that the next time you're in a group of strangers, you'll say hello first to just one person. If that's too much, ease yourself in, by walking into a room and smiling at people.

Practice
The trick is to keep practising being more outgoing – in other words, to fake it until you make it. If you speak to one person at one event, try speaking to two people the next time, then three, and so on. In time, you'll become outwardly less shy despite the anxiety you may still feel within.

Where to get help
If your social anxiety is preventing you from making friends and enjoying your life, please speak to a trusted adult or visit your doctor. They may suggest you'll grow out of it, and they're right – people do tend to become less shy as they mature – but help is available now.

REBEL WITH A CAUSE

Do you always follow the rules? What if the person who made them was wrong? Whether you like rules or not, there can be times when choosing to rebel and go your own way is a wise move

Rules and expectations are a part of life but occasionally it can seem like there's someone telling you what to do and how to behave everywhere you look. Rebelling against convention and pushing boundaries is a big part of exploring your own identity – some people like rules, feeling they make things clear and safe for everyone, others dislike them, finding them petty and stifling.

Whatever your view, making sure you understand why a rule is in place before you follow it is always a good idea – unwise people can make rules too. And rebellion doesn't have to be aggressive or upset those around you. It can be about opposing things you feel are holding you back, like being able to speak your mind; trying to change habits that have a negative effect on the environment, such as encouraging others to use fewer plastic products; or about lifestyle choices that you want to make for yourself, maybe what you want to eat, wear or how you want to spend your free time.

Find your voice

One easy way to rebel is to notice what your friends are wearing or doing and choose to go your own way and do what you want. It's about asserting who you are and being proud about it. Don't be afraid to say what you're feeling, either – voicing an opinion when you see something you don't agree with is a classic trait of rebels throughout history. Just remember to avoid offending others when you speak out – everyone is entitled to their own ideas and beliefs.

Food for thought

Close to half of all vegans are now aged between 15 and 34. If you've chosen not to eat animal products you may find that some people question your decision. Most older people, for instance, have grown up with meat and dairy products being a normal part of their diet and may regard your choice as rebellious and you as 'difficult'.

Whoever makes the family meals may also find it tricky to meet your tastes if the rest of the family eats meat. If that's the case, try to help out with the shopping, preparing and cooking some of your own meals – that way you'll be taking responsibility for the choices you make.

Hot topics

Religion and politics are thorny issues in many homes, but it can be extra difficult if you're the only one in your family with a particular point of view. Or perhaps you've decided not to follow your family's religion? These are big issues, so try to explain the reasons behind your decisions as clearly as you can while remembering to respect that other people's views are as valid as your own.

Party time

Sometimes parents and teachers try to lay down rules that they think will protect you. Age 12, you might be mad keen on gymnastics or tennis, but by the time you reach 15 you may find you're only interested in going to parties and hanging out with a large group of friends until late at night. Parents might consider your new behaviour risky as you could find yourself in a difficult situation that you aren't equipped to deal with, but as far as you're concerned, you want to have fun with your friends and not feel like the one who's missing out. Just try to remember that the choices you make have consequences and keep hold of your common sense.

Best interests

It's normal to want to be free to make your own decisions and live your life the way you want, but if you're going to be rebellious make sure it's in a way that actually benefits you. Rebellion isn't about fitting in with people around you and doing things your parents will get upset about. It's about acting with passion and following your own beliefs, even when that doesn't feel like the easiest choice.

QUIETLY DOES IT

Not all rebels are associated with acts of violence, many activists challenge society through peaceful means to bring about change for the good that affects generations to come.

When **Marley Dias** (*born 3 January 2005*) was 10 years old, she was an avid reader. But as an African-American, she became frustrated that so many of the books she was reading at school were 'about white boys and their dogs'. Determined to do something about it, she launched a campaign called #1000BlackGirlBooks in November 2015 with a simple goal: to ask people to donate 1,000 books that feature black girls as the main character, so she could share them with schools and libraries across the US. Her campaign was so successful she has now collected more than 9,000 books.

Sophie Scholl (*1921-1943*) was a founding member of the non-violent anti-Nazi resistance group The White Rose. The young German and fellow members of the group supported active resistance to Chancellor Adolf Hitler's regime through an anonymous leaflet and graffiti campaign. In February of 1943, she was arrested for handing out leaflets at the University of Munich and executed.

Malala Yousafzai (*born 12 July 1997*) was living in a peaceful valley in Pakistan when the Taliban took control of the area. When they forbade girls from going to school, Malala, aged 11, gave speeches and began blogging for the BBC asking what right they had to take away her education. As her popularity grew, the Taliban issued a death threat against her, and in 2012, while riding a bus home, Malala was shot. She survived and went on to inspire Pakistan's first ever Right to Education bill.

Ryan Hreljac (*born 31 May 1991*) was six years old when he learned from his teacher at his Canadian primary school that children in a Ugandan village had to walk miles each day for fresh drinking water. He started raising funds to pay for a well in the village, and his project grew into the Ryan's Well Foundation, a non-profit water charity that today brings water to people in developing countries across the world.

DON'T BE A SHEEP

It's time to break free from the flock and let the real you flourish

You've probably heard the saying about someone being 'a sheep' and you probably know it's not referring to them being a cute ball of wool bleating around fields. Being a sheep is a term that describes someone who mindlessly follows others in what they say or do. So, are you one?

Most people would like to think they're not influenced by others, but at times it's difficult not to be. Think about your peers at school. How many wear similar clothes, have the same brand of phone, style their hair the same way or start using words or language they've copied from others? Of course, it could be because they simply like this style, but often they're subconsciously following what is deemed to be in fashion rather than actively thinking about what they really want or like.

Of course, there's nothing wrong with copying others if you like their style or you're both drawn to the same things. But if you're following their lead to be accepted or respected, now's the time to make a change and be proud of the real you. It could be that secretly you'd love to go for a different look to those around you but think your friends would laugh, so you hide that part of you.

Copying doesn't only apply to clothes or particular items, though. For some it means imitating the behaviour of friends in order to fit in, even if that involves being mean to other students when you know in your heart it's wrong.

If you feel like this, you're not alone. Here are a few tips to help you feel brave enough to be yourself and embrace the things that make you special.

Who are you?
It's easy to be led by others both in and out of school and to end up trying to be someone you think others want you to be. But what do you honestly like? Are you really a label addict when it comes to clothes or gadgets? What music do you want to listen to? Forget what your friends have playing on their headphones – think about what makes you happy.

Actions speak loudly

Apart from your image, what about your behaviour? It's easy to copy the language and character traits of others until they become a habit and then part of you. Do you treat people a certain way because that's what other students do? Are you judging someone based on others' opinions rather than forming your own? If you realise you're being unpleasant because that's how your friends behave, take a pause and consider if it's really right – or really you.

Similar thoughts apply if you find yourself in a situation that feels uncomfortable. At some point, there'll be events where your peers will be doing things you don't like or don't want to do. Never feel you have to join in because you fear being laughed at or exiled from the crowd. If they're the kind of people who pressure you into certain situations, it may be time to consider if they're true friends.

Be prepared

It's easy to say 'be brave and strong and be true to yourself' but it can be hard and scary being different to your friends at first, saying 'no' or standing up to others. You know you may be mocked or left out of the group. Rejection is one of society's worst fears so it's natural to be worried. Try to remember that some of the most successful people in the world, such as musician Ed Sheeran, singer Rihanna and even the Duchess of Cambridge, were bullied or mocked for being different or 'weird' in their teens but were brave enough to do what they wanted.

When you're ready to be true to yourself, be prepared for eyebrow-raising and negative responses from peers and have some phrases ready. These might help:

* 'I like this style more.'
* 'Laugh all you want, but I wanted to join this club. You can join as well if you want.'
* 'I like them and that's all that should matter.'
* 'I don't feel comfortable so I'll pass, thanks.'
* 'It's boring to be "normal".'
* 'I'm not a sheep. I have my own thoughts.'

You'll be happier

Many people worry that if they don't follow the crowd or stay in line and be just like others, they won't be accepted. If everyone was just brave enough to be themselves, however, the world would be a lot happier.

Our planet needs more people to lead the way by showing their true colours and being bold and distinct – you could be one of them. Your real friends will support you (you may even inspire other students to do their own thing). Most importantly, you'll feel joyful and less stressed being true to yourself. And in the future you'll be grateful you allowed yourself to be happy rather than a 'sheep'.

GUIDING LIGHT

Behind most successful people, there's a mentor
who helped them along the way

What is a mentor?

You may have heard the word 'mentor' before without being sure what it meant
or how it could relate to you (unless you're thinking of applying to *The Voice* and
need a celebrity judge to guide your musical career). Just as a budding singer or
musician can benefit from a musical mentor, you can benefit from a life mentor.
Most people have someone they can turn to when they're struggling with
emotions, worries or concerns and if you find the right person, it can form the basis
of a long-lasting and special relationship.

A mentor is someone you respect and can treat as your go-to person when
you want help or advice, or just need to vent your frustrations. They should be a
trusted adult who can act as a guide, giving you the benefit of their experience
without underestimating your knowledge or dismissing your concerns.

A mentor doesn't need to be someone from the same background as you – they
could have a very different life experience – but what they should be able to offer
is a sense of perspective on matters affecting or concerning you now. A minor
problem can sometimes turn into a major one if ignored, so talking it over with
an impartial person who you trust can help you to find creative solutions.

WHO COULD BE YOUR MENTOR?

A teacher
Is there a tutor you have a good relationship with? Maybe it's because they teach a favourite subject, they're approachable, have a great personality or because they're good at seeing things from your point of view. Start by asking for advice, and they'll most likely be happy to help.

A family member
It can be hard to approach your parents if you're facing a problem. You may not want to worry them, or you may feel they wouldn't understand. Having a mentor who's part of your extended family could be good, especially if they're not directly involved. It could be an older cousin, maybe, or an auntie or uncle, or even a grandparent. Although your grandparents' experience may seem very different to yours, take a chance and they might offer a fresh perspective on a problem that seems impossible to solve.

A family friend
If a friend of your parents has a career you're interested in, why not approach them for advice and ask how they got started? They could tell you what skills and personality traits you need for the job, explain the best ways into the industry, and give you ideas about what you could be doing now to impress potential employers of the future.

A neighbour
It might be that a neighbour has a good knowledge of a subject you're struggling with, for example, a foreign language they speak fluently. Check with your guardians that it's okay to approach them before asking the person politely if they could help you to practise pronunciations without the embarrassment of trying them out in class.

FAMOUS MENTORS

Some of the most influential people in history were encouraged to succeed by a mentor:

* Steve Jobs, who co-founded Apple, helped to guide Facebook's Mark Zuckerberg.
* Mother Teresa, mentor to so many, was herself encouraged by Father Michael van der Peet, whom she confided in many times over the years.
* Greek philosopher Socrates taught Plato, who in turn mentored Aristotle, who went on to tutor Alexander the Great.
* Marie Curie, one of the most influential physicists in history, was greatly influenced by French physicist Henri Becquerel.

BEWARE WHAT YOU SHARE

Sharing on social media can be fun, but some things should never be posted – you never know who might view them further down the line

Sharing is a good characteristic to have, but how much sharing is too much when it comes to social media? We live in a world where people share EVERYTHING online. No doubt you have a friend who updates their statuses or stories several times a day with images and details of their current joys and sorrows... or just to pout at the camera. It could even be you do it, too.

But there are certain things you should be careful about sharing, especially if you're adding people you don't really know.

THINK TWICE BEFORE POSTING...

...your home address

You'd think this was common sense, but some people do check-in at their home address or openly reveal where they live. Criminals find easy targets on social media and will piece together information on unknowing victims about where they live and what items they have that are worth stealing – then, they'll figure out who lives there and when they are and (more significantly) aren't at home. Even more worrying is the fact that some people will post when they are home alone. You may think you know everyone reading your status, but you never can be 100 per cent sure.

...angry talk

You might not like someone or may have had an argument with a friend, but discussing that person and ranting about them on social media could get you into a lot of trouble. If someone sees it and spreads the word, you risk your relationship with that person for good and could also lose a lot of respect from others for airing your personal grievances online. Save your rants for your friends and family, or better still, try to resolve the problem.

...school struggles

When a teacher annoys you at school, it's tempting to be rude about them online. There could be many negative consequences if you do and they find out, however, as you could get in trouble with the school, which might take legal action. The same applies if you have a job and make comments about your boss. You could get yourself fired, so instead of angry posting, talk to a trusted friend.

...posts your future-self will regret

Be wary about being in the images you post and the way you present yourself. Even when you delete posts, future bosses or the police can still find them, so it's best to think twice before swearing, posing for photos that could be embarrassing in the future or posting or re-posting things that could be offensive to others. A good test before posting is thinking if you'd be happy for your gran or a teacher to see or read it. If the answer is no, don't post it.

...holiday highlights

You might be excited to be going on holiday, but it's best not to advertise the fact – otherwise, people will know when you and your family aren't home. Criminals can search the word holiday and check out where you live in less than a minute, so it's better to stay safe and post those beach photos when you get back. If you really need to share, send photos to your closest friends only. Or just use the time to enjoy your holiday instead of being on your phone.

...photos of young children

You may have little ones in your life you look after or spend time with, but always check with their parents before posting photos of them on social media – and this is hugely important when tagging identities. It's always safest not to tag without explicit permission as many guardians really don't want any images of their young children online.

...photos or videos that ridicule others

A random photo or video of someone who's unaware you're taking it might seem funny to you, but remember it's someone's relative, a person who has feelings, and you have no idea of their situation or personal circumstances. The same goes for videos, especially of adults or peers at school. You could find yourself in a lot of trouble for sharing images of people and remember that when you've posted it, others can copy and share it immediately. Even if you decide to delete it five minutes later, you might already be too late.

Final thoughts

To share or not to share? Social media is a great way to keep in touch and connect with those around you, but think: do I really want everyone to see this? Would I be happy with my gran, a teacher, my little cousin or a complete stranger seeing this photo or reading this update? If not, take a deep breath and don't post, knowing you're probably saving yourself a lot of trouble in the long run.

SWEET SOLITUDE

Being alone doesn't have to mean being lonely. Learn how to enjoy solitude and turn it into something you look forward to, rather than dread

Have you ever been in a situation where you've been by yourself, completely content with your own company? Perhaps you've been thoroughly wrapped up in a book or happily rested your head against the window of a slow-moving train, daydreaming. There may, though, have been other times when you've had no one around and have found yourself feeling anxious, unhappy and even panicky. There's a big difference between being lonely and being alone. Being alone is a physical fact, a state of being. Loneliness is a feeling, and not a nice one. It's not a lack of company; it's more the sadness you may feel about that lack of company.

Snacking on social media
When you feel lonely, you might reach out to others. In today's world, that connection is often virtual, via social media or messaging – but actually, this kind of contact can end up causing you to feel even more isolated. Some experts say that seeking relief from loneliness by way of browsing on social media is like snacking on junk food – it fills the gap for that moment but doesn't really nourish you. The other issue is that looking at other people's lives – or at least, the lives they put up on display – can cause you to feel that your own is dull and insignificant. And neither of these things is going to make you feel any less lonely in the long term.

You're not alone
Solitude gives you a chance to spend time with your own thoughts. Sometimes, when you're alone, you may overlook the fact that you do have company – yourself. Choosing to have quality 'alone time' gives you a chance to properly engage with yourself and makes it far easier to cope with the times when being alone is thrust upon you. You don't have to talk to yourself out loud, but those inner chats will strengthen your sense of self and help you to be more secure and confident, whatever you find yourself doing.

What do you want to do?

As valuable as friendships and social connections are, it can be easy to lose sight of your own needs within them. Maybe you want to watch a particular film, but everyone else wants to see a different one. It could be that you're not in the mood for a crowd, but someone has gone ahead and invited a whole gang of people along. When these things happen, you might find yourself going along with other people, rather than causing a fuss or taking care of what you want.

If you find yourself feeling lonely every time you're alone, you're likely to seek out company – but if you learn to love being alone, you can see it as an opportunity to do things that you choose to do. This in turn can make you feel really good.

Filling the space

Throughout history, artists, writers and thinkers have found solitude to help them – the lack of distraction from other people has given their creativity space and freedom. Turning on the TV or watching YouTube videos on your tablet might be one way to forget feelings of loneliness but, like social media, the effect can be hollow. This is because loneliness stems from a desire to connect, while TV and social media only give the impression of this connection. So, it's better to try to connect with yourself. How? That depends on you and what you enjoy doing.

Lonely all the time?

What about if your feelings of loneliness are always there, rather than just happening when you're occasionally alone? You can still use these tips to help you feel more comfortable about solitude and to build your confidence about seeking out people with similar interests and passions to you – by joining a group or club, for example.

You're enough

As American philosopher Wayne Dyer said: 'You cannot be lonely if you like the person you are alone with.' These are wise words. Learn to be your own best friend – after all, you are wonderfully, uniquely yourself and you are lucky to know you. It's about getting truly comfortable in your own company and enjoying spending quality time there.

TIPS FOR ENJOYING 'YOU' TIME

Go for a walk or a run. Venture out somewhere safe and go headphones-free and connect with the feeling of your body, breathing and strength. Not only will you clear your head, but the happy 'feels' released through exercise will keep a smile on your face for hours afterwards.

Find a comfortable space. And then let your mind wander. Allow yourself just to 'be'. Recognise and accept your thoughts and feelings as they come and go, even the negative ones. It's just you, so you don't need to explain anything to anyone.

Get lost in a book. Whether a new release or a comfortingly familiar favourite.

Go outside to a safe space. Time in nature allows you to soak up its sights, sounds and smells. A deeper relationship with the world around you helps you to be more aware of yourself and your place within it.

Get creative. Writing, drawing, customising a piece of clothing, creating a mood board for your dream bedroom. Lose yourself in an activity you enjoy and watch the time fly by.

100 FRIENDS AND COUNTING

Having lots of friends might make you feel popular, but keeping your social circle small can be healthier and have more advantages...

It's easy to feel competitive and obsessive about the number of people in your social circle, particularly when it comes to social media. Those who are seen to have lots of friends and 'likes' are looked upon as the cool, popular ones, who are successful and socially accepted. It seems like everyone wants to hang out with them, be connected to them or follow them on social media, which can give the impression of being adored. When you don't have 20 friends let alone a few thousand, it can feel like you don't fit in and give the false impression of being a social outcast. Having a wide social circle is often mistakenly associated with self-worth and giving a sense of belonging, which is why all kinds of feelings of inadequacy can arise when you don't have as many friends as Mr or Ms Popular.

How many friends are enough?

No one has hundreds of close, personal friends. It's almost impossible to form meaningful friendships with a large number of people. Robin Dunbar, an anthropologist and evolutionary psychologist, and author of the book *How Many Friends Does One Person Need?*, suggests we can engage and form stable relationships with a total of 150 people (including family, friends and acquaintances) at any one time and at varying levels of connection. Out of this number, less than 10 per cent might count as relatively close friendships.

In fact, most people can count the number of their closest friends on one hand and, on average, having three to five dear friendships is considered a healthy number. Some have fewer than three good friends and others have a few more than five, and that's perfectly fine, but the best and most nourishing social circles tend to be small.

So, if you're worrying that your friendship group is small or you're comparing yourself to those on social media who appear to have thousands of connections, rest easy. You really don't need that many friends, nor is it possible to give your full attention to building meaningful friendships with more than a handful of people at a time. Remember that connections on social media may not be a reflection of true friendships.

JUST A FEW GOOD FRIENDS

* It's not how many friends you have that counts, it's the quality of those few good friendships that truly matters. Rather than spreading yourself thinly among too many people, having a small social circle means you'll have time to devote your energies to building mutually enriching friendships, which make for significant and fulfilling relationships.

* There tends to be more trust and loyalty among a few true friends. It's easier to share confidences and life's happenings when you know each other so well. Through shared experiences come the most precious memories and friendships that tend to endure and sometimes even last forever.

* By choosing a small circle of friends, it's likely that you're being true to your needs to create fulfilling friendships with people who truly matter to you.

* Keeping your social circle small means you spend less time spreading yourself thinly and have more time to nurture your number one best friend – you.

'A TRUE FRIEND NEVER GETS IN YOUR WAY
UNLESS YOU HAPPEN TO BE GOING DOWN'

Arnold H Glasgow

Joy of keeping your circle small

If you can count your good friends on one hand, that's nothing to be troubled about – it's cause to celebrate. In many ways, it shows you're secure in your self-worth, recognise the value of quality in your relationships and realise it's far better to have a few dear friends with whom you have a wholesome connection than lots of superficial friendships where you have little in common. Keep in mind that some friends might only be in your life for a short time. Perhaps the friendship was formed out of a mutual interest that you no longer share or it might be you used to live in the same street when you were very young or sat next to each other in class for a year. When life changes, friendships can change, too, unless each party wants – and makes the effort – to stay in touch. If you're lucky, you might have one or two golden people that will stay at your side and share much of your life's journey. These kind of close friends are real treasures and worth an army of casual friends who don't really care.

No matter how long your close friendships last, respect, honour and enjoy the time you spend together. Those moments will always bring more meaning and happiness to your life than being able to say you're number one in the social media popularity stakes.

JEALOUS VIBES

The green–eyed monster can strike at any time and, if left unchecked, it can end up ruining relationships with family and friends. Here are a few things you can try to stop envy from turning into something more destructive

Envy is a regular thing. You might envy what someone has, like a top-of-the-range tablet, or what they appear to be, super cool and original with a life that seems way more glamorous than your own (at least it does on social media). Envying what someone has is one thing, but it crosses over into jealousy when you start to have negative or spiteful feelings about the person who seems to have what you want. When you feel jealous, you might sense that someone or a situation is threatening something you value highly, like a friendship or any relationship that you don't want to lose. It's common to feel jealous if you think you need to compete for someone's attention. Jealousy affects both boys and girls although the latter, who are sometimes more open and in touch with their emotions, are often perceived to be jealous, regardless of whether or not that's the case.

Extreme jealousy can make you feel angry, anxious and threatened. It can also destroy relationships and lead to depression. So it's important to think long and hard as to why someone or something is making you feel bad about yourself. If you believe that a close friend or sibling is more popular, smarter, funnier or better looking than you, it can make you turn against them for no good reason.

They could have been a great friend and emotional support to you for years but suddenly, you start to feel that it's not fair that they have what you want and that, somehow, they are better than you. The reasons will vary but it's important not to let jealousy get the upper hand.

'JEALOUSY IS ALL THE FUN YOU THINK THEY HAD'

Erica Jong

Who's best?

Comparing yourself to others in terms of 'who's best' is
a dangerous game to play as there'll always be someone
who has more than you – even if it's just more likes on
Instagram. The key is to focus on what you have rather
than what you don't have. So if you're jealous of someone's
sporting or academic ability, try to turn it into a positive thing
and use it to motivate you. Work on improving your own skills and developing
your own talents rather than focusing on theirs and don't let jealousy destroy
what was otherwise a perfectly good relationship.

   Try to remember that no one is perfect and no one has a perfect life, it's all
about how you perceive them. The person you believe everyone wants to be like
because they're the most popular one in the group might just be the loudest or
the most outgoing. Another way to look at it is that they might be a show-off,
desperate for attention, or they might just be quite bossy and want everyone
in the group to do exactly what they want. Over time, people may tire of them
because they're quite demanding. Quieter, more introverted types can often
be overshadowed in a group of friends, but that doesn't mean they're any less
interesting or aren't valued.

Jealous of you

Jealousy can also be a problem if someone is treating you in an unpleasant way because you're the one who's the high achiever at school or popular socially. Being on the receiving end of someone's spiteful behaviour is upsetting as it can make you feel guilty for doing well or for being liked. Jealousy sometimes comes from self-doubt or feelings of isolation, so if someone is acting in a jealous way when you get the top exam grades or do well at sport it may not be because they particularly dislike you. They might be angry with themselves for what they perceive as their own lack of academic or athletic ability. It's probably best not to lash out at them – either face to face or on social media – as this may make the situation worse. Instead, try to highlight something they're good at and praise them for it. It can become a problem if so-called friends are continuously spreading jealous rumours or teasing you unnecessarily. If the situation doesn't improve, the answer might be to move on.

Instead of sticking around to let them torment you, you could consider cutting them loose and find a new group of friends to hang out with. After all, true friends would never make you feel bad about yourself.

Coping with jealousy

* Focus on what you have rather than what you don't have.
* Turn any negative thoughts into positive self-motivation.
* Don't let jealousy ruin a good friendship.
* Realise you can't control what others think of you.
* Remember that no one's perfect and difference is exciting.

FACE THE SPOTLIGHT

You might not be someone who naturally wants to be the centre of attention, but sometimes it's good to be seen – and heard. Here, one student shares how she overcomes her fears and anxieties when all eyes are on her

Finding yourself in the limelight can be an uncomfortable and scary place, no matter how many times you've been there and done it before. Whether it's speaking out loud in class or performing on stage, the knowledge that all eyes will be on you can cause a feeling of panic and even put you off doing things in the first place. You might want to take a role in a play, for instance, but the knowledge of how nervous you'll feel when the time comes to perform makes you back off. At the same time, you don't want exciting opportunities to pass you by and neither do you want to come to regret not having pushed yourself a little.

The important thing to remember is being in the limelight is a skill and, like most skills, it needs to be developed and built on. It's likely it will be useful for your future work to become more comfortable with the fact that people will be listening to you, so try not to be afraid of being seen or heard. My position as a deputy head girl involves a lot of public speaking and I also take part in our school's drama productions. This doesn't mean I don't get nervous. I do. But there are a few strategies that help me to be less scared of being in the spotlight.

HOW TO CONQUER THOSE NERVES

Start small
Set yourself a challenge to get out there and give it a go. As much as you don't want to, it might give you a new wave of confidence. Try practising by yourself in front of a mirror or a select few family members or trusted friends. Performing in front of people you know can help and guide you in a positive way. Practice is key to feeling better prepared and more confident about any task.

Be honest – let people know you're worried
Making sure someone knows you're nervous or scared can help relieve the pressure on you as it can make the spotlight a more comfortable space. And knowing someone is proud of you – no matter what happens – is a thought that can give comfort when you're nervous about messing up.

Are you ready?
Feeling like you're 'ready' can be difficult to know. But the more you believe you can speak in public or play a role, the less likely you are to be nervous. If, however, you're approached about a role you really don't think you're ready for, you can say, 'no, thank you, not this time'. This gives you space to identify where you need to build your confidence for the next opportunity that comes along.

Take a minute

Having self-belief can improve your performance and daily life dramatically. In the moments before putting yourself in the limelight, allow yourself a little time to relax, take some deep breaths, and repeatedly say 'I can do this' in your head – it can really help with nerves and the butterflies in your stomach. Even if you don't believe it, you can 'fake it till you make it' as they say.

Carry on

If something doesn't go to plan, keep going. People will forget what may have gone wrong (if they even noticed) and focus on the good parts. Carrying on means you're brave and tells the audience you believe you can impress them. It's also worth saying to yourself: 'We're all human and we all make mistakes'. It's through this that we learn, and people can sympathise with that.

'TAKE CHANCES, MAKE MISTAKES. THAT'S HOW YOU GROW'

Mary Tyler Moore

Join a club

Joining the school debating team or drama group can help build your confidence because you can be in a team and help each other out. Tell the group leader you want to increase your confidence and ask for tips or support. You could perhaps consider going to an open mic night near you to watch what happens and see how other people perform. You could even think about having stepping up yourself.

Know your stuff

Properly understanding and having a real passion for what you may be performing or saying means you can feel more confident about having people watch or listen to you. It means there are fewer things for you to worry about. When performing, 'knowing your stuff' can take that weight off your shoulders and give you the energy you need to overcome any nerves. You can do it.

SUNSHINE BREATH

Yogic breathing exercises have the power to energise both body and mind.
Here we take a closer look at the *chin mudra*...

If you take a moment to notice your breathing as you go through your day, you'll
see it can make a difference to how you feel. Stop every now and then, think about
your breath and practise inhaling more deeply, all the way down to your stomach,
especially at times when you're feeling worried. Do you feel calmer, more relaxed?
This exercise is perfect for connecting your thoughts and your breath.

Sit in a comfortable seated position on the floor with your hands gently resting
on your knees, palms facing upwards, or in a mudra position, where the first finger
and thumb are touching. This is called *chin mudra*.

In yogic science, each part of the hand connects to a certain area of the brain.
When you apply pressure to the fingers and hands, those brain areas are
energised. The *chin mudra* activates wisdom and knowledge.

Breathing gently, take a moment to allow your body and mind to settle.
Then slowly close your eyes and imagine a big, bright, shiny, hot sun.

Now to begin the breathing exercise:

1. Take a deep breath in, all the way down to your stomach, for a count of three.
    As you are breathing in, picture a big, bright, shiny hot sun. Hold this image in
    your mind's eye for a count of two or four, whichever feels most comfortable.
2. Then gently breathe out for a count of six and as you breathe out imagine you
    are that big, bright sun, radiating light out into the world.

Repeat this breathing exercise for three to five minutes and observe how your
body feels. You may feel warm, energised, light and glowing afterwards.

Younger children should be supervised.

FESTIVAL OF FUN

Let your creativity run wild as you organise your own special summertime event

During the summer months, festivals seem to pop up everywhere. Some, such as Glastonbury, revolve around music. Others celebrate arts, films, literature or health and wellbeing. Despite their popularity though, it's not always possible to travel to these large-scale events or actually get your hands on a much-coveted (and increasingly expensive) ticket. So, if you want to attend a festival this summer, why not organise your own?

Choose a theme

One of the first things you need to consider is the theme of your mini-festival. Do you simply want to listen to your favourite bands via Spotify and pretend you're dancing in a field at a festival, or would you prefer an event dedicated to wellness, crafts or a much-loved film? Perhaps you're passionate about an issue, the natural world for instance, and want to highlight the importance of climate change. Or maybe you're eager to raise money for a local animal shelter, so your festival will have a caring-for-animals theme – the options are endless.

Decide on a name

It can be great fun deciding what to call a summer festival, so explore a few options before settling on a name. If you want to avoid any ambiguity, go for something straightforward such as 'Carrie's Arts and Crafts Festival'. If you're organising the event with a friend, you could combine your names to make up a brand new word, for example 'KateJo'. The Lollapalooza Festival that takes place in seven countries around the world got its name because the word means a thing or person that's particularly impressive, so you could always study a thesaurus or pick up a French or Spanish dictionary for inspiration.

Be imaginative. If the festival is taking place in your garden, could 'Daisychain 2023' be a possibility? Incorporate the name of your favourite hero, the street where you live, the song that makes you smile – just be sure you're happy with your choice. If your festival is a great success, it could become an annual event.

Once you decide on a name, you may also want to design a logo or even put together a flyer or booklet – organising a festival really is an opportunity to let your creative talents shine through.

Plan the entertainment

Next up is thinking about how you will entertain everyone on the day. Consider the size of your venue and the number of people attending and try to link as much as you can back to your festival theme – it should help to influence the music, what you eat and drink, as well as the all-important dress code.

Are you keen to have a programme of activities and events and stick to a timetable? If so, you could allocate an hour at 2pm to learning circus tricks, for example, balloon sculpting at 4pm, acrobatics at 5pm, with everyone then participating in a grand finale. Or maybe you just want to do as you please with no time constraints. Is it important to display information about a local charity or good cause to prompt discussions, or create a chillout area that anyone can retreat to? It's entirely up to you. Don't be too ambitious though, and definitely don't fret. Ultimately, your festival is all about having fun with your friends and no doubt as they arrive they'll all have suggestions on what you can do.

Get creative

Festival planning allows you to reveal your inner artist, especially when it comes to designing invitations, banners or wristbands and VIP lanyards (or straps) for festivalgoers to wear. Decorating your setting is enjoyable too. Collect glass jars in the run-up to the big day and pick a few wild or garden flowers to arrange in them (remember to leave enough for the bees, though). A string of bunting sewn from scraps of material can also help to transform a tent or garage into a pretty festival venue. Solar fairy lights will look wonderful at night. And why not seek out a wheelbarrow and fill it with ice to keep drinks cool? If you love baking, show off your skills and make cupcakes for everyone to eat or create a garden bar with citrus punches and homemade smoothies. Be original when thinking about toppings and ingredients – could these also link back to your theme? Clever, innovative ideas will be the talk of your festival and make it the event of the summer. Hopefully you'll make plenty of great memories too.

Remember
* Ask permission before organising your event.
* If you're planning to hold your festival in your garden, let your neighbours know.
* Have a Plan B. Any outdoor fun will come to an abrupt stop if it starts to rain.
* On a hot sunny day, provide somewhere for people to sit in the shade.
* Don't advertise your festival on social media. You may be excited about hosting an event, but you don't want your whole school to turn up.
* Make sure you have plenty of rubbish bags to collect any litter.

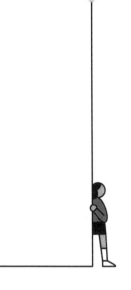

THE STUPIDITY OF CONFIDENCE

It's all too easy to avoid situations that could lead to embarrassment – but the key to feeling confident is to know that you'll always make mistakes. Be brave and put yourself out there

Confidence isn't a talent that some people are born with and others don't have. It is, however, a bit of a skill, like whistling or touching your toes. But unlike whistling and touching your toes, the trick to being confident is in the mind. It's about knowing that you'll never be perfect and accepting that there are times when you'll make mistakes. Many people who lack self-confidence avoid situations where they could potentially make an error or end up feeling embarrassed. You might want to join a sports club, for instance, but don't because you're afraid of being rejected or looking stupid in front of teammates.

You might worry that the coach of the sports team will think you're not good enough or that you'll hold others back. But in truth, the only real skill you need for confidence is the ability to look foolish and not care. Yes, you may not quite be good enough to make the team, but at least you tried. At some point you will make the team – and if not that team, then another. But if you never put yourself out there, you'll never make it.

You're not alone

It's easy to compare yourself to people that you admire. It may seem like they don't make the same dumb and clumsy mistakes that you do. They appear luckier with friends, more sure-footed or, you may think, more remarkable. You may admire those cool and confident people for their ability to so effortlessly do the things that you're unable to. The trouble with this belief is that it is almost certainly not true. Everyone is aware of his or her own faults and flaws, after all, you wake up with them every day and they nag at you whenever you want to try something new. What you won't see, however, is the doubts and anxieties of the people you admire, which are hidden away. You might imagine that you're a rare ball of anxiety and nerves, and that you're the only one feeling this way – but that's untrue. All of those feelings are shared with the rest of the world. Everyone is hiding his or her own fears – some people are just better at covering it up.

Will people notice?

Consider what drives a fear of looking stupid – is it a fear of what other people will think of you? Well, British philosopher Alain de Botton summarises this nicely in a blog post on theschooloflife.com. 'Remember that only some hate, a very few love – and almost all just don't care,' he says. It's something to bear in mind. While you're worrying about what other people think of you, the chances are they're doing the very same thing. That is, they're just as worried about other people's opinions as you are – and that means they're not going to spend time thinking about your slight mistake because they're focusing on their own.

What's more, the idea that people would find you less appealing for showing that you're a human being with flaws is incorrect. It's been proven that those who ask follow-up questions after an explanation, rather than just saying that they understand, actually come across as more confident than those who don't. Try not to worry if you're unsure about something, and don't be afraid to admit it and ask questions. People will think more of you just for allowing yourself to look like you don't know.

Are you underestimating yourself?

So if you want to become a more confident person, it helps to wake up every day and tell yourself that you're a bit of an idiot! It may seem like strange advice, but if you accept that you will do stupid things and make mistakes each one is easier to deal with. If you remember that you, along with everyone else, are prone to looking stupid, then you never have to worry about looking stupid again.

If you lack confidence in your ability, take comfort from a study that showed 'stupid people' are more likely to rate themselves higher in an intelligence test. Research undertaken by psychologists Justin Kruger and David Dunning in 1999 showed that the less intelligent a person is, the more likely they are to rate themselves as capable. It also found that people who really are competent are more likely to underestimate their skills. So, if you doubt your ability, it could mean that you're actually pretty smart, you just don't know it. Don't let that go to your head, though. A bit of modesty is never a bad thing.

SOAR LIKE AN EAGLE

This yoga pose stretches the shoulder and upper back, increases breathing capacity, and strengthens the thighs, hips, ankles and calves

Eagles are admired as symbols of power, freedom and transcendence. They're strong, proud, noble creatures with amazing eyesight: they can spy prey three kilometres away, see in five basic colours (for humans, it's only three), and detect ultraviolet light. The eagle pose, or *Garudasana* in Sanskrit, is a standing balance pose that develops focus, strength and serenity. Students with knee injuries are advised to follow the alternative option as described in our top tips below.

Here's how to get into the pose:

1. Stand strong and proud in mountain pose – aim to be tall and upright, with your chest out and shoulders down – feet pointing forwards and arms falling beside the body, with palms facing forwards.
2. On an in breath, raise your arms in front of you up to shoulder level. Keep the palms facing upwards.
3. Cross your left arm over your right. Bend your arms at the elbow and wrap your forearms around each other, bringing your palms together pointing upwards.
4. On an out breath, bend your knees and shift your weight onto your left leg.
5. On an in breath, cross your right leg over your left thigh, and hook your right foot around your left calf.
6. Hold this position, breathing in and out, slowly and deeply.
7. On an out breath, release your arm and legs back into mountain pose.
8. Repeat the pose, beginning with your opposite arms and legs.
9. If you practise this pose regularly you'll be able to observe how your balance, focus, strength and serenity begin to soar.

Top tips

* To assist balance in this position, focus your gaze on a point in front of you.
* Use a wall to brace and support your back while learning to balance.
* It can be difficult to maintain balance on the one foot. An alternative option is to cross the legs but, instead of hooking the raised foot behind the calf, press the big toe of the raised-leg foot against the floor to help with stability.

DON'T STOP THE MUSIC

Learning to play certain instruments, a trumpet for example, might be deemed uncool by some students and make you want to stop. But here's why sticking with it could be one of the wisest choices you'll ever make...

Unless you're a child genius who can play the piano like Beethoven, you probably first picked up an instrument at primary school. If your lessons were anything like mine, the music room was filled with the sounds of tooting recorders, clashing symbols, tinkling triangles and whistling flutes for the first few years. The guitar seemed too hard with its six strings and tricky chords, and the drum kit in the corner was almost impossible to master without hours of practice.

But one musical instrument stood out to me. It was gold, shiny and had bouncy buttons that popped up and down when you played it. It also had a huge bell that amplified any note that was blown into its polished little mouthpiece. Every sound that came out of the end was loud and proud, like a fanfare, and made me feel like I was opening a circus or starting a march. I fell in love with the trumpet there and then. I was eight years old. I started lessons in my lunch break and joined the school band, performing at summer fairs and Christmas plays. I'll be honest, being on stage in front of a crowd – even though it was mostly made up of teachers and parents – felt pretty cool. It was as close to a pop star as I was ever going to get (I'm not very good at singing).

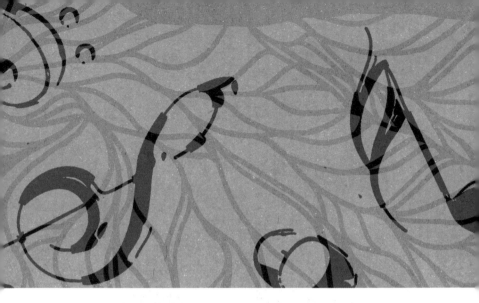

What's cool for school?

I kept practising and playing, playing and practising, and after a couple of years I decided that I wanted to be a professional musician. When I was old enough, I was going to play my trumpet all over the world. That was until I started secondary school, then everything changed.

Apparently playing the trumpet wasn't cool at my new school. People laughed at the clunky case I carried around the corridors, calling me a 'geek' and a 'nerd'. They mocked my decision to sign up to the orchestra and giggled when I played at big events like sports tournaments and presentations. Even tooting my trumpet at the school concert caused people to point and laugh. But here's the thing, I kept on playing. I stayed proud, stuck to my lessons and made sure I became the best trumpet player I could be. My favourite musical instrument had given me so much joy up until then, I couldn't give up on it now. It still gave me that same powerful feeling I first experienced aged eight when I felt like I was welcoming the queen to town. What I realised was that after a few years I would never have to see those name-callers again, I could carry on doing what I loved and maybe even perform on stages across the globe – I just had to choose my path and not let people I didn't even like change my hopes and dreams.

Star power

Actually, playing this shiny brass instrument is cool. There are plenty of talented musicians who have sold millions of records that feature the trumpet. Ask your parents or grandparents about Louis Armstrong or Miles Davis, two jazz legends who built their entire careers around the cheerful parp of a trumpet. In fact, without the brass instrument the whole genre of jazz might not have even existed. The more you think about it, the more you notice trumpets toot up in lots of songs by the world's biggest stars. Jay Z has tunes that feature the instrument, so does Pharrell Williams – and a Beyoncé concert commonly features girls playing trumpets galore (check out Crystal Torres who also writes, sings and plays her own songs). If pop music isn't your thing, there are lots of other opportunities to play the trumpet – Alison Balsom is an award-winning musician in the classical field. You could also be a session musician, playing live with rock bands or on studio albums; join a wedding band and watch people dance to your music all night long; or, you could sit in the pit at the theatre and play along with famous shows like *The Lion King*, *School of Rock* and *Matilda*.

Carry on playing

The point is, instruments are awesome. Without them, music wouldn't exist. So, if you're thinking about quitting just because someone else doesn't like the instrument you love, don't. After all, somebody's got to stand next to Beyoncé and play the trumpet – and that person could be you.

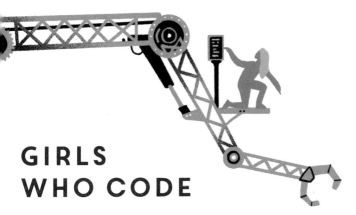

GIRLS
WHO CODE

Coding is the language of the future – it's easy to learn, fun to use to make your own website, game or app, and could even help you win your dream job

It's a typical scenario. The local sixth-form college is holding interviews for new students. There's a queue of boys waiting to talk to the computer science teacher and a line of girls ready to sign up for courses in childcare. Why? The truth is many girls just don't see themselves writing code for apps, games, websites or IT systems – if that sounds like you, you're missing out on something that can aid all-round brain power, increase career prospects and be fun. Amali de Alwis is the head of Code First: Girls, an organisation that aims to get more women coding and working in the world of tech. It runs courses for over-18s but Amali would like to see more girls getting involved: 'Some people think if they haven't done it since the age of six they've missed the boat,' she says, 'but that's absolutely not the case. There's lots of help out there to set you on a journey that will give you a good career at the end.'

Golden ticket
We're not talking about ending up in a boring office fixing other people's computers. Coding is a versatile skill that can be applied in all sorts of jobs – entertainment, games, manufacturing, retail, healthcare and more. Amali says it's important to look at its real-world value rather than its geek appeal.

'One of my students is now an instructor. She first came in wearing boots and funky clothes and stuff. She was working for a company that sold wool, and she was sitting there knitting saying: "This is what I'm doing when I'm writing computer script – I'm following a set of instructions which is telling me how to create a pattern and get a certain outcome at the end."'

'IT ALWAYS SEEMS IMPOSSIBLE UNTIL IT'S DONE'

Nelson Mandela

Where to begin
There are plenty of ways you can get involved, either online or through after-school clubs and summer school workshops, often for free or at little cost. 'There are lots of free sources online,' advises Amali. 'We recommend platforms like Codecademy, Dash and Code.org, which have content ranged by age from as young as three or four all the way through.'

Blazing a trail
The results can be fast, too. One student, Funmi, completed the Code First: Girls beginner's course and a little over a year later was already working as a junior developer at mobile phone app banking service Starling. Another student, Jess, took the beginner's course in 2015 and is a software developer for global technology consultancy ThoughtWorks. According to the Office of National Statistics in 2017, only 3.9 per cent of people working in tech were female programmers and software developers, so any girls who do have a go at coding have the chance to be trailblazers for change as well.

SO WHAT'S IN IT FOR ME?

* Coding experts widely agree that it can improve mental agility, everyday communication skills, problem-solving, creativity and logical thinking.
* A sense of satisfaction: rather than playing something someone else has created over and over again, you can make something new of your own.
* It builds confidence in exploring the wider digital world of apps, games and web design.
* There are social benefits from joining coding clubs and after-school groups and meeting people with a similar interest and sharing ideas.
* It can mean more money when you go to work: research by Tech City UK found that tech jobs pay 36 per cent more than the national average.
* You will be in demand: London tech giants have committed to creating one million tech jobs by 2023.

HOW TO GET STARTED

Codecademy. Offers free coding classes in a wide range of different programming languages and HTML. *codecademy.com*

STEMNET. Helps young people and teachers access STEM Clubs (science, technology, engineering and maths) and links with STEM Ambassadors. *stem.org.uk*

Dash. Online self-learning site to get the basics of web development for beginners, including HTML and Javascript. *dash.generalassemb.ly*

Kids Ruby. A fun way to learn the Ruby computer language through creating games and other simple programs, with a split screen function that shows what the code says and what it does. *Kidsruby.com*

Hopscotch. Step-by-step interactive learning app, available for iPhone and iPad. Aimed at students aged 10 and over. *gethopscotch.com*

WANT TO BE A YOUTUBE STAR?

Then you might want to think again. Here's why there's more to life than a YouTube career – even for those who are living it...

YouTubers make people laugh, comfort them and inspire them. They can also give viewers something to aspire to – who wouldn't want to make a living from vlogging about things they're passionate about, right? But just because the lifestyle seems desirable doesn't mean you shouldn't question what it means to be a YouTuber, and whether it's really what you want.

When YouTube becomes a job, it has pitfalls and challenges like any other. There are endless opportunities for jobs and careers out there if you stay openminded and explore your hobbies, talents and dreams. You don't need online fans to be happy and fulfilled.

Being good enough

One of the biggest draws of a YouTube career is that it's such an easy platform to get into. With camera equipment and editing software, anyone can create a YouTube channel. You can script your videos, stick to an upload schedule and update your social media to match. But what if you don't become popular?

No one is ever guaranteed to be successful online. There isn't a formula – and while there are no certainties in life or in any job, it's important to remember that your worth isn't connected to how many online followers you have. Professional YouTubers are under constant pressure to maintain their subscribers and large audiences. If their number of views starts dropping, it can be tough to ignore thoughts that they aren't good enough.

External validation comes from other people praising you and your decisions, or in this case watching and praising your videos. It might feel good for a while, but it wears off quickly, and you might find you start to feel down about yourself until the next time you're praised. It can be addictive, and it's never enough.

Validation from yourself is stronger and more valuable. Inner confidence – accepting who you are and taking care of yourself – is a healthier and kinder aspiration than popularity, and can last a lifetime. You can learn to rely on yourself, not online followers.

Always happy?

It's easy to believe that YouTubers are always content – but it's fairly straightforward to make yourself appear happy online. Vlogs seem candid and casual, but that doesn't mean that YouTubers don't pick and choose what you view. Often, they want the internet to see only the best side of them. No one feels their absolute best every day and it would be unfair to place that expectation on yourself.

Being a professional YouTuber is a full-time career like any other. If you want to be successful and remain at the top of your game it takes hard work and requires passion, long hours and a willingness to persevere through difficult times. It's also useful to remember that YouTubers are people with fully rounded lives. They have friends and hobbies they might not post about on YouTube, and they have bad days and times when they feel upset, but you may not see that on their channel.

Many YouTubers have acknowledged how their career affects their lives – both the positives and the negatives. YouTuber Zoe Sugg, aka Zoella, wrote on her blog that she overcame anxiety with the help of a therapist and her friends and family. It wasn't her YouTube career that helped her – it was hard work and support, and at the time this was all happening, she wasn't letting it show on YouTube.

One friend of Zoe's is fellow YouTuber Louise Pentland (aka SprinkleofGlitter), who has written on her blog about the pressure of high internet standards. 'For a long time I've tried to be perfect. It's exhausting,' she said, before going on to acknowledge that her YouTube channel did not reflect her authentic self – messy hair, ups and downs, and all. Now, Louise sets out to make videos that reflect her whole self, but it took many years for her to feel confident enough to do so.

The real deal

It's easy for YouTubers to feel the pressure of having to be happy and high energy all the time, but real happiness is more valuable than looking happy online.

Popularity on YouTube has its positives, but it's good to consider the negatives too. Finding something that fulfils you, rather than something that may make you popular, will give you genuine happiness.

WHAT JOB WILL MAKE YOU HAPPY?

A job that matches your interests is more likely to keep you smiling. Use these ideas as the starting point to work out what your dream job might look like

I am a great communicator
Think about work that will allow you to persuade other people to do something, buy something or believe in your cause.

I am practically minded
Look for something hands-on, like building, cooking, working with animals, plants, and machines, sports or hands-on therapy.

I love to make new things happen
Search for careers that will let you achieve things. This may involve planning, managing projects, leadership and organising teams of people.

I want to help and support people
Think about jobs that mean you'll be working with people, putting their wellbeing and development at the forefront. Charities, healthcare, education.

I like to research and manage information
Focus on work that includes analysis, cataloging and managing databases, IT, science, quality control or researching topics in depth.

I want to use ideas creatively
Working imaginatively with ideas or designs could include jobs in film, TV, photography, publishing, also business creativity, marketing or architecture.

FICTIONAL FRIENDS

Bookmark a few fantastic reads with special characters inside

Whether you're an avid bookworm or someone who reads now and again, a good book can encourage you to be brave, be kind, be extraordinary or just be yourself. Books take you on adventures to destinations you've never visited, introduce you to people you've never met and even allow you to get up close to creatures that would be impossible to imagine without a vivid description. Books can teach you about history, influence your opinions and inspire you to achieve great things. No wonder people often say they make a big impact on their lives.

And taking centre stage, there is always one captivating character with the capacity to make you laugh, cry, ponder new ideas and motivate you to discover and learn more. As you turn the pages, these characters become your friends, and for as long as it takes you to reach 'the end', you get an intimate insight into their lives, thinking, goals and dreams. With that in mind, which characters in classic books and contemporary novels do you think would make the best fictional friends? Here are a few of our suggestions...

Beatrice Prior

Strong, brave and fiercely independent, Beatrice Prior, or Tris, is the smart protagonist in the *Divergent* series of books by Veronica Roth. Not one to toe the line, especially in the dystopian future she finds herself in, Tris demonstrates remarkable courage and stands up for what she believes to be right. You couldn't ask for a more considerate and caring friend, as she regularly thinks of others before herself – even if that puts her own life in danger. Days would never be dull if Tris were your friend. Be prepared for daredevil antics.

Jem Finch

In the thought-provoking *To Kill A Mocking Bird* by author Harper Lee, Jem Finch is the older – and devoted – brother of six-year-old narrator Scout. Their father is a lawyer and the siblings soon learn about racial discrimination in 1930s Alabama and are witness to people's prejudices. Jem loves getting up to mischief and would definitely make you laugh out loud, but he's a kind boy too. He understands the importance of justice and telling the truth. It would be easy to follow his example and lend a hand to others who are fragile. Jem would get your folks' approval.

Cameron Ann Morgan

A student at the Gallagher Academy for Exceptional Young Women, Cammie Morgan appears to be no one special, blending in with the crowd. That's one of her skills as a spy and with the code name The Chameleon it's to be expected. As you'll soon uncover while reading Ally Carter's *Gallagher Girls* series of teen novels, share a classroom with Cammie and you'll be learning martial arts, computer-hacking tricks and how to be fluent in 14 languages. Intelligent, witty, compassionate and fun to be around, Cammie is perfect friend material – but don't be tempted to share any of her secrets.

Hermione Granger

If you ever need proof that anything is achievable if you're determined and work hard, look no further than Hermione Granger, the magical muggle of JK Rowling's *Harry Potter* series. One of the bravest students in Gryffindor, Hermione is a high achiever who hates letting anyone down. As a friend, she's as loyal as they come – and with a wand in her hand, she could be a valuable asset if you find yourself in a tight spot. A word of warning: if you don't fancy getting up close to a Hungarian horntail or Dementor, maybe it's wise to hang out at home.

Josephine March

Creative and carefree, Josephine, or Jo as she prefers to be called, is one of four March sisters in *Little Women* by Louise May Alcott. Shunning the conventions of 19th-century society, she refuses to behave in a gender-stereotypical way and appears boisterous, perhaps even obnoxious at times. A genuine friend would see underneath this façade and realise that Jo's a sensitive soul, a lover of literature who wants to be accepted for who she is. Anyone would find her enthusiasm and ambition infectious – and agree that you don't always need to conform to be a success.

Liesel Meminger

The Book Thief follows the life of the young, yet determined Liesel Meminger. As the title suggests, Liesel loves reading and because she's living under Nazi control in 1939 Germany, where many books have been banned, she has to steal reading material. Few of us would want to go through the same hardship as Liesel, witnessing immense cruelty first-hand. But Liesel, perhaps more than others, is in need of a trustworthy friend. Her bond with a Jewish man hiding in her foster parents' basement illustrates her kindness and humanity and this powerful novel, written by Markus Zusak, proves that true friendship gets you through the good times, and the bad.

Your favourites

Are you in awe of Katniss Everdeen of *The Hunger Games* fame and want a slice of the action too? Or are you bowled over by Maria Singh's determination to fight racial discrimination and gender stereotypes in *Step Up To The Plate* and want her on your side? Pick up a notebook and write down the names of any book characters who you think would make a great friend and, in a few words, say why.

SEE FOR YOURSELF

There's no right or wrong way to look at art, and no right or wrong way to think about it. But there are a few things that can help you to understand what an artist is trying to say

It wasn't so long ago that the only way you could see artwork was on a poster, in a book or by making a visit to a gallery yourself and seeing the real thing up close and personal. Today it's much easier. All you have to do is reach into your pocket, take out your phone and with a few touches on your screen you can discover whatever artwork you like – without even having to get off the sofa.

When you're viewing pictures on a small, shiny screen, however, you're looking at a reproduction that has lost some of its power and impact. In a gallery, knowing that the image presented before you is the one true original that the artist created with their own hands all those years ago can be awe-inspiring. That artwork is the masterpiece that all those postcards, posters and images on the internet come from – it's a powerful experience.

Here are some of the things you might like to keep in mind when exploring the wonderfully rich and varied world of art...

Be prepared

Visiting a gallery website beforehand will give you a taste and prepare you for what you'll see when you go to an exhibition. It also gives you time to find the answers to any questions you may have, especially if some of the pieces feel complicated or confusing. You're more likely to enjoy the art if you have a greater understanding of it.

Find something that interests you

While researching your chosen exhibition, find a few artworks that grab your attention and raise your curiosity levels. You can then look for them at the gallery. It gives more of a purpose to your visit and it's a great feeling to stand in front of a work of art – painting or installation – you'd been reading about a few days before.

Be open-minded

It's rare that you'll like absolutely everything you see in a gallery. Often, the work people don't like is talked about more than those that they do. As long as a piece has made you feel something, then its job has been done. Some artists seem to enjoy being controversial. When the public first saw a piece called *Mother and Child (Divided)* by Damien Hirst in 1993, it left many asking how two cows displayed in tanks of a chemical called formaldehyde could possibly be considered art. But it drew people to visit the gallery to see what the controversy was about.

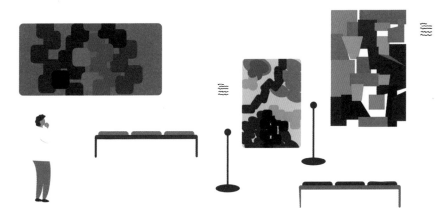

Take your time

There's a tendency to rush around a gallery – to try to cram in as much as possible. Try not to feel pressured to move on if your friends want to see what's next or if other people are jostling behind you. Take your time and go at your own pace so that you don't miss the artworks that would have touched your soul if only you'd had longer to look at them.

Look and read

As well as the artwork, there's often written information on the wall or in handouts. This can give context about the work and explain something intriguing that might not be obvious from just looking at it. When looking at *Rain, Steam and Speed* by J M W. Turner, at first it seems like an unfinished painting of a train crossing a bridge. It becomes more interesting when you discover that before creating the painting, Turner deliberately stuck his head out of the window of a speeding train in the middle of a storm to experience the steam, wind and rain for himself. Knowing the context of the piece helps you to realise that the apparently scruffy way in which the artist painted *Rain, Steam and Speed* represents the turbulent weather and the elements. You begin to feel like you're there.

Get up close

Step forward and take a close-up look at the details within the artwork. This might offer clues about the artist's techniques and why they've used them. Vincent van Gogh was known for creating landscape paintings that could express powerful emotions. One of the ways in which he accomplished this was by the thick, rapid, physical brushstrokes within his work. When you stand close and see the individual brushstrokes in *Starry Night*, you begin to see how Vincent created his painting mark by mark. You also get an insight into a troubled and passionate man who put his heart and soul into his paintings. *Starry Night* was created while he was recovering in hospital after experiencing mental health problems. It was based upon the view from his window.

It's always okay if you don't understand it

Some artwork is supposed to challenge you and make you ask lots of questions about it. That's the great thing about art. It can make you think – not just about the piece in front of you, but about the world you live in and life generally. Sometimes when new artwork is first unveiled, even the experts are confused by what they're seeing.

In 1907, when people first viewed Spanish artist Pablo Picasso's early geometric work, which saw humans represented as a collection of shapes and angles, they didn't like it, but that was partly because they didn't understand it. They couldn't comprehend that the artist was experimenting with a whole new visual language called Cubism. A language that, like many of Pablo's paintings, looks modern and fresh even today.

MAKE A VISION BOARD

Creating a vision board can help you frame and reach your goals, from what you want to do today, to who you want to be tomorrow...

What is a vision board?

A collage of inspiring pictures, words and quotes that represents you, your hopes and dreams. It's a great way to map out and see more clearly your short- and long-term goals at school and in your life, whether that's what career you hope to have, or things you'd like to change or do right now or next week.

How will a vision board help?

It can be easy to lose sight of your goals on a day-to-day basis. You may write them down one day and then forget all about them until you find the sheet of paper in a drawer months later. Creating a board allows you to display them somewhere that's permanently on view, where it can serve as a reminder and an inspiration. Deciding what to include on your vision board can also be a good mindfulness exercise. If you feel like you're being pulled in different directions, are under pressure at school or have some difficult decisions to make, then creating a board can help you to take a step back and see the things that are important to you more clearly. The great thing about making this board is that there are no rules when it comes to gathering your images, wording and quotes.

81

Breathe

You will need:

* A base for your vision board, which could be a piece of card, a cork board or even some cardboard from an old cereal box.
* A happy photograph of yourself.
* Scissors and a glue stick, or get crafty with washi tape and some colourful pins.
* A variety of magazines and pictures that you don't mind cutting up. You can always go online and find images that your magazines don't include, as well as photos of friends, family and pets.

SIX STEPS TO CREATE YOUR BOARD

1 Set the scene for the next couple of hours by finding a quiet, comfortable spot. Turn your phone off and put your favourite music on.

2 Ask yourself what you would choose to do if fear didn't exist and you knew you would succeed in everything you did. How would your life look? This is an important question to ask because you don't want to limit any of your goals – nothing is out of reach when you're putting together your vision board.

3 Cut out any pictures, words or quotes that make you feel good and inspire you. There are no rules when it comes to what you want to express. A picture could include a school sports team you want to join, a favourite flower you think is beautiful, a role in a play you hope to be chosen for, a new skill or hobby you'd love to take up, a country you'd like to visit, influential figures you look up to, people you love and things for which you're grateful – anything goes.

4 Focus on personal goals and dreams, relationships in your life, the relationship you have with yourself, your hopes and aspirations. Keep in mind the bigger picture – fundamentals like health, love and happiness rather than the newest phone, fashion fad or celebrity you'd like to look like.

5 Try to organise your collage before you stick it down. As you place the pictures on the board you'll get an intuitive sense of how the board should be laid out. For example, you might want to place the picture of yourself in the centre, and assign a theme to each corner of the board. Maybe short-term school goals could go in one corner, with long-term career goals in the opposite corner. Everyone is different when it comes to their personal board, so just go with what feels right and have fun.

6 Leave space on your board so that there's always a place for accepting new things into your life. Take time to refresh the board when images have served their purpose and goals have been reached.

BEDROOM BLISS

Your bedroom and the way you decorate it can say a lot about who you are. Here's how to revamp your room so it truly reflects your style

Transforming a tired, drab and uninviting bedroom into a feel-good retreat that is uniquely you might seem like a challenge. In fact, all it takes is a little imagination and resourcefulness to give your 'mini-apartment' an inspiring makeover. Start by considering what style, theme and colour scheme appeals. Do you prefer a cool, peaceful space or one that's warm and vibrant? How will it reflect your personality? Do a sketch of your room and draw up a design plan. Decide what you'll need and work out how you'll keep it to a budget.

Once you've considered the design and practical elements, discuss the plans with your parents. Talk to them about what changes you'd like to make and why it's important to you. Listen to their perspective. A bedroom re-design can be costly, but they'll be more supportive and enthusiastic if you explain ways to minimise costs by upcycling what you have or using pre-loved finds. Be creative and take your time. Focus on preparing your canvas first (walls, ceiling, floor) and then let your own style emerge naturally.

MAKEOVER TIPS

* Design your room with multi-purpose in mind. Create zones where you can rest, study, chat, to friends and prepare to face the world.

* What music, films and books do you enjoy? How do you spend your leisure time? Are you passionate about a certain era, culture or place? Let your interests inspire your style.

* If you have changeable tastes or are unsure about what you want to achieve, choose a neutral colour, such as white or cream, and make a statement with boldly coloured pictures and accessories.

* In her book, *DIY Bedroom Decor: 50 Awesome Ideas for Your Room*, Tana Smith explains: 'One of the simplest ways to dress up your room is by adding lots of fun and trendy decorations to your walls.' Arrange picture frames in a novel way. Use wall-hangings and decals, aka transfers, to display your favourite quotes or images.

* Re-purpose existing furniture to fit your theme. Change dull drawer handles and light shades for vintage finds. Re-paint an old wardrobe or chest to complement your new colour palette.

* Choose a mix-and-match of textiles for bedding, curtains, throws and cushions. Different patterns and contrasting colours add interest, particularly to a room with a neutral tone.

* Don't forget to decorate your ceiling. On the interior design blog, greenandmustard.co.uk, Anna Tonkin sees the ceiling as the fifth wall. She says: 'How fabulous to look up and see a marvellous delight of colour, from sunny yellow to the deepest darkest grey.'

* Be open to ideas from family and friends, but let your bedroom reflect your signature style and be somewhere you can really relax. After all, you're the one who'll spend the most time there.

WHAT'S YOUR STYLE?

Bohemian
If you're free-spirited and have diverse tastes, choose an eclectic mix of styles. Add a riot of colour and patterns. Choose intriguing pictures and ornaments. The effect might look quirky, but it'll be original. Boho styling means 'anything goes' as long as you love it.

Dedicated space
Perhaps you're a music fan, or love nature or sprinting. Whatever your interests, make sure your room reflects them. An old gig T-shirt could become a focal point, plants might express a relaxation zone, while motivation could be found in framed photos of 100m Olympians.

Scandinavian simplicity
The classic Scandinavian style is perfect if you love a cosy, calm and bright space. From floor to ceiling, white is dominant with a hint of colour to provide warmth.

Minimalist
If you like your space clean, cool and clutter-free, think functional. Make a bold impression by using a limited colour palette, such as black and white. Store belongings out-of-sight and keep surfaces clear. Less is more.

Fairy-tale whimsical
Inspired by tales of happy-ever-after and enchantment? Make your room dream-like. Hang shimmering voile curtains and choose cushions and accessories featuring foxes, hares, owls, dragons and other magical creatures. Display found treasures and favourite fairy-tale books on a rustic shelf.

Vintage chic
Travel back in time. Is there an era that inspires you? Is it the glam 1950s, rebellious 1960s or over-the-top 1980s? Or do you have an affinity with Victoriana? Give your room the retro treatment and embellish with vintage memorabilia. Check out vintage stores for treasure.

THE CLOTHES SHOW

Choosing what to wear to a party can be fun, but it might also feel a bit scary. After all, clothes can equal judgment day and a dressing-down from the 'fashion police'. There are, however, ways to take a kinder look in the wardrobe and develop confidence in your own original style

Perhaps some things about growing up don't seem all that much fun (increasing amounts of homework, for example) but one of the best things about it is increased freedom. And not just in terms of doing things and going places, but also in terms of what it means for self-expression.

This applies to several things – bedroom decor, for instance, or music choices. It also applies to choosing and wearing clothes but, unlike a bedroom, which only family and friends might get to see, your style sense and fashion choices are visible to the eyes of many. For some people, the thought of being judged on the basis of an outfit choice can be intimidating. After all, clothing makes a statement about

various aspects of your life and personality and not everyone's comfortable with these being on show and up for evaluation and discussion.

What kinds of assumptions might be made on the basis of clothing? There are labels such as 'cool' and 'uncool', as well as judgments such as 'showy' and 'scruffy'. It's not uncommon to judge a book by its cover and to make certain assessments based on very little – and those who do so (which is quite a few) aren't necessarily being unkind, whether their judgments are correct or not.

You could assume that someone on the bus wearing a suit is going to work in a smart office, for example, or that the person wearing an Arsenal T-shirt is a football fan. Even so, knowing that these assumptions are being made means that not everybody feels at ease with putting a statement about themselves out there for all the world to see.

This is especially the case if you're still experimenting and finding out who you are and what your style is. It can be hard enough to feel comfortable and confident as it is without feeling others might be making judgments and labelling you based on what you're wearing that day.

Wear it well

School uniform, for those who wear it, helps to reduce these issues on a day-to-day basis, but what about occasions like own-clothes days and parties? For some students, these might represent a chance to experiment and take a break from the norm, but for others they could seem horribly exposing. What to wear? What will everyone else be wearing? What will people think – and say?

The first thing to remember is that how something is worn has far more of an impact than what exactly those clothes are. As the international fashion designer Diane von Furstenberg once said: 'Confidence. If you have it, you can make anything look good.'

That sounds like an easy thing for a person who is designing and wearing beautiful clothes to say, but the meaning behind these words is that the people who are truly comfortable and happy in what they are wearing are far more likely to have that enviable ease and self-assurance than someone who's wearing something that doesn't really reflect their personality or taste. It's this that makes clothes look good, not the other way around.

CONCERT 18.00

YES OR NO

Freedom of movement

This doesn't just apply to being fashionable or not. It also concerns practicality and fit. Having to constantly tug a top down or a strap up isn't only annoying for the wearer, it will probably make them look irritable and ill at ease too. Shoes that are too high or too tight make for an awkward walk and uncomfortable day generally, while a shorter skirt may look great while you're standing, but be a bit trickier to sit or bend in. It's a much better idea to take into account what an occasion has in store – dancing, running, sitting cross-legged on the floor, being indoors or outdoors – and then opt for clothes that allow freedom of movement and comfort in the circumstance.

In all likelihood, many of your friends and peers are feeling exactly the same, even if they don't always show it. If humans could see through walls, they'd probably glimpse hundreds of bedrooms with clothes pulled out of drawers, tried on, and then thrown onto the floor! So-called grown-ups are just the same, frequently worrying about what to wear to dinner, an interview or dress-down Friday at work. It can be reassuring to talk to a friend before, say, a party or event, about what they're planning to wear, or even to plan your outfits and get ready together. A trusted perspective from someone who knows you well can be a great confidence booster. Don't be afraid just to have fun and be yourself and to remember that an outfit you love today may get shoved to the back of the drawer next month. Trends change and so do personal tastes and favourites. It's all part of finding your own style and experimenting with different looks as you go.

SAY IT YOUR WAY

If a teacher's request to put an author's idea or a scientist's study
into your own words sends you running for cover, you're not alone.
It's a skill that can be difficult to master, but it's an important one –
and not just for schoolwork

Putting someone else's ideas or information into your own words – also called paraphrasing – is an essential academic skill. Copying something directly from a book, website or classmate in an official school assignment or exam can lead to accusations of plagiarism (cheating). The consequences can be severe – and might even include disqualification from an entire course.

But it's not just about avoiding getting into trouble. Putting something into your own words helps you properly to understand the content, which is one of the reasons that you're often asked to do it.

Simply copying from another source doesn't take much effort, but rewriting requires you to engage with what you've read or listened to. You have to make sense of it in a way that's meaningful to you, then create your own interpretation. It's a longer process, but more valuable. And, if you truly understand something, it's likely to make future classwork, assignments and exams much easier.

Your unique voice

The skill isn't only useful at school, either. Perhaps you've found yourself repeating the exact words you've read or heard elsewhere when chatting to friends in person or online, or debating in class. There's not necessarily anything wrong with this – indeed, sharing posts is encouraged on social media – but if you've not completely understood the original, it might mean you're repeating views and opinions that you don't actually agree with, but which others will then attribute to you. You might, for example, be repeating something hurtful, without even realising it.

It's super-easy to copy-and-paste when working on-screen, or to write down, word-for-word, what a classmate has written. And it's not always about saving time. You might simply believe an author or academic has expressed things so well that there's no way you could improve on it or there's no other way of saying it.

However, putting ideas into your own words is always worth the extra effort and, as with many things, the more you practise, the easier it becomes. Next time you're faced with this task, try some of the ideas over the page to help get you started.

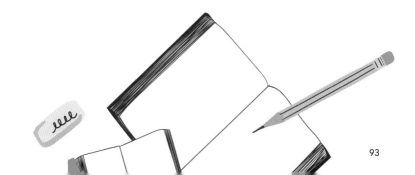

OUTSIDE THE TEXTBOOK

If you're asked to write something in your own words for an assignment, see if any of the following work for you:

* Read the original text carefully several times, remembering to look up the meaning of any unfamiliar words. Then cover it up. Now imagine that you're talking to a friend, sibling or parent, explaining to them what you've just read. It doesn't matter if you don't have a real listener. Just speaking aloud this way can help you to structure your thoughts before putting pen to paper.

* If you have a photocopy or printout of the original text, try crossing out all except the key words of each sentence. You might leave in important words, such as scientific vocabulary that you don't want to forget. Now rewrite the piece, using just your key words as prompts, to remind you what to include in each sentence or paragraph.

* Try putting the original information into a different form. For example, turn what you've read into a quick drawing, comic strip, diagram or flow chart. Next, cover the original text and use just your illustration to help you rewrite it in your own words.

* It can be impossible to express something in your own words if you've not really understood the information in the first place. So, if you're struggling to get to grips with what you're reading, try looking for more straightforward information to help explain things. Although the internet is a great research tool, remember that most websites are written for older people. Seek out websites, books, videos or podcasts made specifically for younger age groups (such as BBC Bitesize). Using several different sources of information will deepen your knowledge and make it easier for you to produce your own work.

AND DON'T FORGET...

* It's usually fine to copy something word-for-word as part of an assignment if you quote your source (the book or website you found it on). Usually, you'll have to state the author and book title or web address, so remember to make a note of these when you're doing your research.

* Ask for help. Teachers, parents, librarians, older siblings and friends can all be good sources. They might be able to explain a topic to you or help you find information that's easier to understand. Remember, there's no such thing as a silly question.

* Don't compare your work with the original text or with a classmate's. Your teachers want to know what you've understood. Putting something into your own words, even if you're worried that yours aren't as good as somebody else's, helps your teachers to resolve any misunderstandings and give you more constructive feedback.

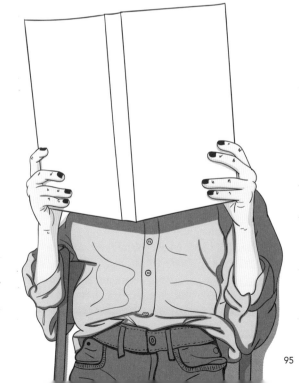

'I LEARNED TO
WRITE BY WRITING'

Neil Gaiman

SEEING DOUBLE

Have you ever looked at your friend and seen... yourself? Same hairstyle, clothes, even mannerisms? If so, you probably have a copycat friend. Here's how to address the issue or even curb your own copycat behaviour...

Copycat friends can sometimes be difficult to cope with – so much so that you might be considering breaking off your friendship. Before you do that, however, it might help you to know that imitation is something most people do to some degree throughout their lives.

It can be a particularly common habit in teenage years, a crucial stepping stone in establishing identity and personal taste, but sometimes continues into adulthood. Your parents' friends probably don't dress like them, but they might, for instance, decide to decorate their homes similarly or book a holiday to the same destination. At its core, emulation is a way of establishing a sense of belonging. It's almost like a glue that bonds friends together, helping them recognise each other as part of the same group. The message copycats are sending, even if they don't realise it, is that they share your tastes and interests

and want to be part of your set. As child psychologist Amanda Gummer, founder of Fundamentally Children, explains: 'We are all social beings, with a powerful desire to fit in. When children start becoming independent from their families, they search for other groups to belong to and friends are an obvious focus. Teenagers will often go through a phase of copying someone they like or admire, primarily as a means of being accepted by that person.'

Even though there may not be anything sinister or scary in copycat behaviour – in fact it's actually a compliment, since your friend is only imitating you because they think you're amazing – it can cause tension in friendships.

Individuality is important, so when a friend tries to be like you, it's understandable that you might feel they're compromising the qualities that make you unique. It may get to a point where you want to confront them about their copycat behaviour, but bear in mind that they might be acting like this because of their own insecurities and lack of self-confidence. If you're going to broach the subject with them, you should try to do it with some sensitivity.

On the flip side, you might be reading this and thinking about your own behaviour. It could be that you feel you're struggling to find your voice and define your tastes, and you're therefore adopting someone else's. If this sounds like you, try to take steps to develop your own way of dressing and behaving and think about what you like doing, watching and reading. It might be hard to begin with, but the only person you can most successfully be is you.

WAYS TO COPE WITH A COPYCAT FRIEND

View the problem from a fresh perspective
Before making any accusations, consider the situation from different angles, and seek the opinion of someone you trust. Try not to involve a group of your classmates, since this is likely to make the situation worse. Could it be that your friend isn't really copying you? It might be that you both like the same clothes, but that doesn't necessarily mean they're copying your style. It may be no more than coincidence that they've bought some of the same things as you. Make sure you're interpreting the situation correctly before talking to them.

Find something that interests you
If you're convinced you're being copied and feel you have to question them on their behaviour, be tactful. Bear in mind that the root cause could be insecurity, so don't belittle them or call them out in public. Instead, try to boost their confidence. You could say that you'd noticed they'd bought some of the same clothes as you, but that they might look even better in another colour or style. You could even suggest you go shopping together and help them choose items different to your own. Your friend might be copying some of the things you post on social media without giving you credit. You could explain, calmly, that you put a lot of thought into your posts and you don't feel it's fair that they're passing them off as their own.

Find something that interests you
Be prepared for your friend to carry on copying even after you've spoken to them. If it just so happens that they like the same things as you, it's unlikely talking to them will change anything. In some cases, then, it might be better to accept being copied as part of growing up. Sooner or later your friend will find their own identity. Until that happens, you can rest assured that no one can really be you but you.

HOW TO STOP BEING A COPYCAT

Developing a sense of self is an important milestone and part of that is establishing your own likes and dislikes. But if you're constantly borrowing your friends' preferences, you might struggle to establish your own distinct identity. When you're next out clothes shopping, take a step back before you buy something your friend has already. Ask yourself first if you really do like it, and second, if it's a style that genuinely suits you. You may then be left asking yourself why you feel the need to copy that person. Does it make you feel more confident or closer to them? In time, most young people grow out of mirroring, and begin to trust their own judgments and tastes. When this doesn't happen, the reason might be low self-esteem – and then it's a case of taking the steps necessary to boost that sense of self-belief. Always be the best version of you.

'ALWAYS BE A FIRST-RATE VERSION OF YOURSELF, INSTEAD OF A SECOND-RATE VERSION OF SOMEONE ELSE'

Judy Garland

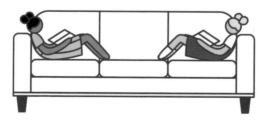

LET'S PARTY

Want to celebrate your special occasion in style? Here's how to throw the ultimate big-day bash

Planning is key

Organising a party can be just as exciting as the main event. You could get creative in the preparation stage by mapping out a colourful brainstorm or putting together a mood board to include all your ideas. Are you ready to put some of your thoughts to paper? Set aside some time, grab a notebook and pen and get planning. You might want to consider some of the top party planning points and suggestions, below.

1 **Location.** Look at all your options, especially ones that don't bust the budget. Instead of hiring a space, use locations that are easily accessible and full of potential – your home, garden or even the local park. If you live near the coast, might the beach be an option?

2 **Guest list.** Always keep your location in mind because the more people you invite the less space you have. Also, it's good to remember that this is your party so invite only people you really want to spend time with, true friends and family.

3 **Theme.** Think of a subject that could connect all the elements of your event. If you can't think of one right now, don't worry. Here are a few ideas we like:

Colour. Theme your party around your favourite colour and choose decorations, food and drink to suit. For the colour yellow, you could choose yellow paper decorations, cheese and pineapple sticks and fresh lemonade. You could even go the extra mile and add the colour of choice to your dress code.

Initial. If fancy dress is your idea of fun, then why not ask your guests to come dressed as something beginning with the initial of your first name. For example, the letter L could include a lion, a lumberjack or a librarian.

Season. Let the time of year inspire you. If your birthday falls in summer, you could opt for a tropical theme, complete with fake flamingos and palm trees. Winter birthday? You could go with a snowy scene or opt for a warm and cosy gathering instead: hot chocolate, brownies and a favourite film.

Era. A decade theme can make for some great costumes and music choices. There's something for everyone here: from the roaring 20s and *Great Gatsby*-style outfits to the hippy era of the 70s and flower power.

Eat, drink and be merry

A party isn't complete without a buffet table covered in snacks. Whether it's sandwiches and cheese straws or chips and dips with crudités, simple finger food makes for a great people pleaser. Going simple on the food means there's more scope to be creative with the drinks. Switch the fizzy drinks for some sophisticated mocktails using fruit juices, syrups and fancy garnishes.

Make a playlist

Think of the type of party you'd like and then compile a playlist that reflects the theme. If it's a summer party, what sun-filled tracks do you know? Make a note of your theme and list some related song titles under it. Get the party started.

A day to remember

One of the most important things about throwing a birthday party is making memories. One way to do this is using a photo booth (see right) to capture snaps of you and your friends together. You could also ask your guests to write a special birthday message in a memory book for you to look back on when the party's over.

Party not your thing?

The thought of throwing (or going to) a big bash is enough to give many people the heebie-jeebies. Luckily, there are plenty of other ways to celebrate. Here are just a few:

* **Go to an ice-rink**. Grab a pair of skates and show off your moves (or cling to the side if you're a bit unsteady).
* **Watch a film and order a takeaway**. Cosy clothes, pizza and a favourite film. What more could you want?
* **Visit a theme park**. The perfect option for adrenaline junkies – buckle up and prepare to scream.
* **Go bowling**. A fun time whether you're competitive or just playing for laughs. Plus, you can dress the part.

HOW TO CREATE YOUR OWN PHOTO BOOTH

Find space. Choose a spot with good lighting and away from your other guests. This will ensure the photos look great and help people feel less self-conscious with the props.

Find a backdrop. This could be anything from a plain wall to a metallic, foil-fringed curtain or coloured fabric – the choice is yours. If your venue is outside, use the natural surroundings as your backdrop.

Find a photo-booth camera. If you have a good-quality camera (and a family member who's willing to take the pictures) that's great, but not essential. A selfie stick and a phone or a Polaroid camera that generates instant snaps are brilliant alternatives.

Find props. Search your home and vintage shops for suitable items that will make for inexpensive and varied photos – feather boas, cowboy hats, sunglasses or tiaras are perfect. You could also create your own using online printable templates.

Get posing. Get your props on and enjoy pulling funny faces and being goofy with your friends.

Get printing. Don't forget to download and print your party pix and remember to give copies to your guests, too. You might want to share the snaps in a dedicated WhatsApp group.

I'D LIKE TO TEACH THE WORLD TO SING

Do you sometimes feel you have a song in your heart but you're not sure how to express it? Here's how to make a start...

Sometimes emotions can hit you so hard you need to find a way to express them – or you might have a tune buzzing around in your head that you need to match with lyrics. Songwriting is a wonderful way to manage your feelings and create something beautiful, and it can feel like you're drawing order out of chaos. Whether you've fallen in love, had a break-up, a fight with a friend or just an amazing experience, a song is a great way to express it. Here, a professional musician and singer gives some advice on how to get started.

It doesn't need to sound like poetry
Some writers are praised for their poetry, others make brilliant songs from words that may make sense to no one but themselves. Who else 'feels like a room without a roof'? Anyone? That didn't stop Pharrell Williams from having a massive hit with those lyrics in his song *Happy*.

You don't have to do it alone
If you can write lyrics but stuggle with music, collaboration could be the key to your songwriting future. Maybe you've got a friend who plays the guitar or piano who could put music to your words? It may take a while to gain each other's trust – but once you do, a level of mutual understanding can yield some truly unexpected results you would never have arrived at alone.

Don't hold back
When I started writing, I would often discard my songs after a couple of lines because I thought they weren't as god-like as those of my heroes. That's a mistake, though. Don't be afraid to be bad. I found that I was only able to improve by exploring my weaknesses.

Don't be afraid to get personal
Generalisations are fine, but they are brought to life by details. Our lives consist of large sweeping feelings and events, in addition to tiny details. Those little details in a song are what tell us we're listening to a human being. If you're struggling to find a way to express an idea, go back to your own favourite music and see if you can fit your lyrics into an established structure. It's a bit like trying to express a poem in the tight form of a haiku – it can force things out of you that you would never have thought of if you hadn't set yourself those boundaries.

But don't forget the rules either
People like to think of art as wild and spontaneous, and it's true that some of the most original breakthroughs have been made by throwing out conventional wisdom and going for something completely off the map. But technique is your friend. Most rule-breakers knew the rules to start with, and even the most seemingly unprecedented piece of work might well be more rooted in the nuts and bolts of craft than you might imagine.

Don't be scared of clichés
You don't want to write someone else's song, but at the same time, clichés became clichés because they're true – and they can be hard to avoid if you are writing about pop's favourite topic: love.

Try a different perspective
If you've turned to songwriting because you're hurt after a fall-out with a friend, try writing a lyric from the other person's point of view. Very few people go around cackling maniacally, revelling in the emotional wreckage of their actions. Most people believe themselves to be the good guy. If you think yourself into the shoes of that other person, you might find you understand their position better. Then again, you might not, but you might end up with a good song at the end of it.

Be true to yourself
Don't bind yourself to pop music conventions – 1970s band Queen didn't in their hit *Bohemian Rhapsody*, but it still held the number one slot in the UK pop charts for nine weeks, and is still featured in films and advertisements today.

SING, SING A SONG

* Pick your favourite song and write a new verse about your own experience.
* Go for a walk, look around you and write about what you see and hear, and how it makes you feel.
* Write a song about a person, either someone real or a fictional character. You could tell their story, describe them or just write how you feel about them.
* Try to write a song that rhymes, then try to write a song without any rhymes at all. How will you make it hang together?
* Write a song in a style of music you wouldn't normally listen to, whether it be heavy metal, country, pop or rap.

EARN WHILE YOU LEARN

Money, money, money. It's difficult to ignore the subject of cash when your pocket money isn't enough to pay for your hobbies, entertainment or an impromptu shopping trip. If you want to be more financially independent so that you don't have to rely so heavily on the bank of mum and dad, here are some original spare-time money-making ideas

Cleaning service
When it comes to cleaning, whether it's washing the car, tidying up around the home and garden, making windows sparkle or even mucking-out horse stables, most people are happy to pay for some assistance. If you enjoy the challenge of making everything look super shiny and new, you can earn from your own cleaning venture.

Dog walking and pet-minding

People sometimes need help with their pets. If you love animals and have some experience of handling and caring for them, why not try offering a dog-walking or pet-minding service? This is a perfect venture if you hope to work with animals as a career.

Weekend job

Is there a local shop, farm, café, restaurant, garden centre or tourist attraction looking for assistance at the weekend? Jobs as a waitress or waiter are quite common and you might earn extra tips, too. This is a great way of learning new skills, meeting people and earning regular income. It's also a step on the ladder to permanent, full-time employment.

Leaflet and newspaper delivery

Do you enjoy walking and keeping fit? You can earn while you walk by offering a leaflet and newspaper delivery service for local businesses and newsagents. You'll need to know your route and be happy to deliver whatever the weather.

Babysitting

If you are patient, mature, friendly and great with children, you might want to consider babysitting. Parents often need a reliable and, of course, responsible babysitter for a few hours on evenings and weekends.

Sell your crafts

Are you good at art, knitting, pottery or making things? Can you write heartfelt or humorous poetry? Offer a service selling your craft. Post a notice in your local shop. Let family and friends know what you do. If you're good at art, you can sell your designs online on a website like RedBubble.com (it's best to check that your parents or guardians are okay for you to do this). You simply upload your images, and they take care of the orders, sales and delivery, and you earn for each item sold.

Become a YouTube star

Like being in the spotlight? If you're good at making videos and have something interesting to share on a regular basis, you can build a YouTube channel. Once you have enough subscribers, you can apply for the partner programme, which allows you to earn advertising revenue from your videos. Do remember, though, that YouTube comes with high pressures. Both Zoe Sugg, aka Zoella, and Louise Pentland, aka SprinkleofGlitter, have written about how exhausting and demoralising it can be trying to maintain a super-successful online profile. If you're 13 or under, you'll also need to have your parents' or guardians' permission.

Earn online

You can actually get paid for visiting websites and completing surveys online. It might not make you a fortune but by completing simple tasks, you earn points, which can be redeemed for gift cards that you can spend at online shops.

Sell things

Do you have a stack of books, CDs, toys and clothes that you've outgrown? Perhaps you have a bike or video games you no longer use. Have a clear-out. Sell unwanted items at a car-boot sale. If you enjoy selling things, find out what's popular and look for car-boot sale bargains that you can sell on for a profit.

TIPS FOR SUCCESS

Promote yourself. Create a leaflet about your services and share with your family, friends and neighbours. If you're looking for a spare-time job, visit local businesses to ask if they have any weekend vacancies or to bear you in mind for future opportunities.

Make a great impression. Courtesy and politeness go a very long way. So, smile! Be positive and helpful. Treat people as you'd like to be treated in return. Set out to make a great impression and you'll likely earn yourself an excellent reputation – as well as money.

Be prompt. Always make sure you turn up on time. Be organised, reliable and keep your appointments. It's better to be early than late.

Make safety a priority. Be safety conscious. If you're meeting someone for the first time, take an adult with you. Always let your parents know where you're going and how long you're likely to be. Be mindful of health and safety as you work. Follow instructions and commit to safe practice. For example, take care when using ladders, make sure you put equipment away so it isn't a trip hazard and look out for health and safety risks. If you're unsure about anything, always ask for advice.

Be professional. Whatever service you offer, do your best. Pay attention to detail and be professional from start to finish. Go that extra mile to show you care about what you do. When you focus on quality, people will use your services again, and that means more money for you.

And your hours? During term-time, children in the UK can only be employed for a maximum of 12 hours a week. This includes a maximum of two hours on school days and Sundays; a maximum of five hours on Saturdays for 13 to 14-year-olds; or eight hours for 15 to 16-year-olds. For further information, visit gov.uk/child-employment.

FRAME, CLICK
AND PRINT

Have you ever taken a picture on an old-fashioned analogue camera, one that uses film? If you haven't, chances are you will soon, because from instant photography to disposable cameras, film is making a comeback

Before the invention of the digital camera (in 1975) photographers loaded their cameras with rolls of film. These rolls were generally limited to 24 or 36 exposures, and once they were used up the film was rewound, removed and sent off for processing. Film cameras didn't have a screen on the back to help you to review your work, so there was no quick way to check if you'd taken a good photo. When digital photography came along this all changed. Today you don't need to buy film, and you don't have to spend money on processing it. You can see your photo the second you've taken it and this makes it easier to share with family and friends. So, why are so many people returning to film? Here are just a few of the reasons why analogue's return to popularity is such great news...

ANALOGUE IS AWESOME

Shooting on film is exciting
The joy of film lies in the suspense between the instant you take a picture and the moment you see the results. Sometimes you feel certain you've captured the perfect shot and you can't wait to finish the rest of the film so you can see it. There's a whole hands-on process that needs to be followed – finish the roll, drop it off at a lab, wait a few days for them to be ready, during which time the anticipation and excitement builds. When you go to collect them, you're filled with hopes and expectations, and sometimes you're disappointed – a head chopped off at the neck, a blurry face – and other times it's like a miracle, even better than you'd imagined.

Film gives fabulous colours
Digital cameras do a great job of imitating the vivid images that film can produce, but film's rich colour palette and dynamic range (mix of shadows and highlights) gives a brighter, more vibrant result. Try taking a photo with a digital camera and then do the same with an analogue one, and compare the two. You might be surprised at how much smoother and more natural the film image looks. Many up-and-coming photographers are switching to film because it can make their photos really stand out.

Film makes you a good photographer
When you take pictures on your tablet or phone, it doesn't matter if the shot isn't great, you can hit delete and take another. Before you know it, you've snapped 10 quick-fire images just to get one good one. But when you have only 24 or 36 frames, and you know that each one is going to cost you money to process, you put more thought into what you're doing. If you're photographing a friend, for example, you spend time checking the edges of the frame for distracting objects such as branches. You make the effort to get the exposure right by analysing light conditions and tweaking the camera controls. And when you're more careful about every photo, you become a better photographer.

'I WANT ONLY TO CAPTURE A MINUTE PART OF REALITY'

Henri Cartier-Bresson

Film helps you to be more mindful

Chances are you have your phone with you all the time, so taking it out and grabbing a quick snap becomes a reflex action. But if you find yourself taking hundreds of images and posting them online without really noticing you're doing it, you're missing out on exciting creative opportunities, and the chance to engage fully with the world around you. Shooting digitally, it's tempting to check the screen after each shot – a habit known as chimping. But checking your screen too often can make you miss out on what's actually happening around you. Shooting with film, on the other hand, encourages you to engage more with your surroundings and live in the moment.

Displaying your prints is fun

Most shots on your phone begin and end as digital files, but there's something magical about holding a print in your hands. Selecting which prints to display in an album or on your wall can make you question why you value one image – or experience – over another, and looking at these images later can trigger the emotions you felt at the time, helping you to relive that joy.

Focusing on one image is better

Photography is all about capturing a single moment in time, and the truest expression of that is with a single image. Look back through the photos on your phone and you'll probably find lots of pictures of the same thing, which can make them all a bit 'same-old, same-old'. Try to take one strong image of important moments, however, and you may really capture that instant.

NOW IT'S YOUR TURN...

If you like the sound of film but don't yet have an analogue camera, why not use your mobile to mimic the old days? See if you can shoot just 24 frames in a week, and don't check the results until the seven days are up. Use the following tips and ideas to give you ideas of what to photograph.

Use natural light. If you're indoors, move your shot close to the window. Make sure the light source is behind you and illuminating your subject.

Take photos of people in an unobtrusive way. Don't say, 'I'm going to take your picture'. People immediately freeze and get awkward. Instead, keep talking with them as you shoot so they act more natural.

Be aware of your background. A wonky horizon can be annoying. Try to frame your shot by taking a picture through overhanging branches or windows, use tunnels, arches or doorways – you can even use people, for example shooting over shoulders or between heads. Your frame doesn't need to go right round the edges of your image – they might just be on one or two edges.

Think about the picture beforehand. French photographer Henri Cartier-Bresson once commented: *'Thinking should be done before and afterwards... never while actually taking a photograph.'* Try to conjure up an image in your mind's eye before you release the shutter.

Helpful hints

* Take photos that say something about who you are – but which don't have any people in.
* Look up or down, there might be something you never noticed before – an architectural feature, interesting shadows or reflections, geometric shapes that grab your eye.

WHAT IS THE MEANING OF LIFE?

Ever felt small and insignificant looking up at a dazzling night sky? Ditto. Perhaps it's time to ponder one of life's big questions...

Have you ever looked up at a clear night sky, lit by millions of stars, and suddenly felt the world is truly immense and that you are insignificant in comparison, or wondered despairingly 'what's the point of it all?' when things don't go your way? The former seems reasonable, the latter perhaps less so. But if you think about it seriously (and in the right mood), the question is actually one worth asking. In fact, 'What's the point of it all?' is one of the most profound debates of human existence. There's no clear answer: some believe life has no purpose, others take the opposite view and argue it's for the individual to discover what it is. Maybe the answer isn't so complex. Maybe the meaning of life is simply to give life a meaning. So, to live happily and make the most of what it has to offer.

As a very young child, you're told what to do and how to behave until there comes a point when you begin to start thinking, learning and making decisions for yourself. This is when you establish your identity and begin to push back adult-imposed boundaries.

The big philosophical questions, including the meaning or purpose of life, also tend to raise their heads. Some consider the ultimate goal to be happiness, but what brings contentment is likely to differ greatly for each person. You might find happiness sitting in your bedroom immersed in a much-loved book while a fellow student would find the activity beyond boring and beg to be allowed out to play football. The answer? Don't try to be like anyone else. Find out for yourself what it is that makes you happy.

Right now, that might be curling up with that favoured novel or competing on the pitch. Going forward, it could be finding a job that brings out the best of your abilities, setting out to achieve long-held experiences or spending time with people you love. Throughout, it's about understanding yourself and the world.

Some people (even seven-year-olds) know exactly what they want to do in life while others (the majority) spend time looking for that special thing that will motivate them. It takes time and experience. Don't beat yourself up if you sometimes feel lost or clueless. Instead, venture out, open your mind, meet people, pursue your passions, discover new hobbies and try to find your place in the world.

Don't be afraid to make mistakes. It's part of learning and, weirdly enough, you need it to get a better sense of direction. But the search for the meaning of life and happiness is as much on the inside. There is a fascinating world in your head and trying to figure out who you are – your strengths and weaknesses, your hopes and fears – is just as important for you to be able to accept your true self and the world and people around you.

Finding your place

Understanding yourself and the world better won't necessarily make you more happy. But it can make you more aware of your potential and what you could do to make a difference, from helping family and friends to suggesting lifestyle changes that will benefit the environment. So, happiness or usefulness? Whatever your goal, it is a personal journey that only you can decide. Answers can come effortlessly, but they can also take time. Perhaps, then, if you live life to the full and appreciate all its little wonders and the things so often taken for granted, you'll begin finally to believe your role in this vast world is significant. You may even understand the meaning of it all… or, at least, some of it.

Want to know what life is all about? Read these uplifting tips from inspiring women…

'There is not one big cosmic meaning for all; there is only the meaning we each give to our life, an individual meaning, an individual plot, like an individual novel, a book for each person'

Diarist and novelist, Anaïs Nin

'What you do makes a difference, and you have to decide what kind of difference you want to make'

Primatologist, Jane Goodall

'You don't become what you want, you become what you believe'

Broadcaster, actor and producer, Oprah Winfrey

'We do not need magic to change the world, we carry all the power we need inside ourselves already: we have the power to imagine better'

Author, JK Rowling

'Life is a fairy tale. Live it with wonder and amazement'

Author, Welwyn Wilton Katz

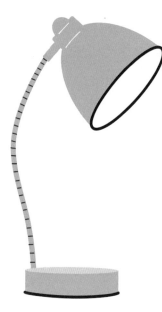

WRITE ON

Don't let hang-ups about grammar or punctuation put you off – writing is good for the soul, and done freely there's no easier way to express yourself

Lots of people let worries that they can't write well enough stop them from putting pen to paper. Yet writing is for everybody. It's free. You can do it practically anywhere and you don't need special equipment. And the amazing thing is that everyone has their own voice or style of writing. Given the same first sentence, each person would come up with a completely unique piece of writing. Introducing a little bit of writing into your day is a great stress reliever too. You have to concentrate just on the page, in the moment, putting one word after another, building sentence by sentence, paragraph by paragraph. Before you know it, you've written hundreds of words. And you can be proud of having created something from nothing. Getting your thoughts down on paper can also help stop them whirring round and round inside your head. You can express feelings, frustrations, work through sadness or anger or write down the things you wished you'd said to somebody, all in the privacy of your own notebook.

JUST BEGIN

So what are you waiting for? Let's get writing...

First, why not give yourself a break from screens
and pick up a pen or pencil instead? There's something
special about connecting your brain to the movement of your hand and
the formation of letters. A very different sensation from typing. Dig out that old
fountain pen for a change, or use bright felt-tips.

You don't even need to write in lines down the page unless you want to. Try
spirals, or diagonals. Use tiny writing for a small character, MASSIVE letters for a
shouting giant. Play with the words on the page. This isn't homework to hand in.

But I don't know what to write...
When you're free writing like this you don't need to worry about a plot or
creating a 'finished' piece. That can all come later if you decide to carry on working
on something. You'll find your imagination is fired up by certain exercises and
you'll want to spend more time on them, making them into a poem, story
or even a novel. But others may leave you uninspired. That's fine – move on.
Find what works for YOU.

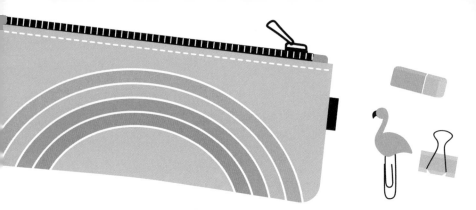

Try the following prompts to get you started:

1 Make a list

You'll be surprised by how much character can be revealed in a list, or how easily lists can turn into mini-poems or short stories. Try these...

* List items in the room of someone you know well to sum up their character, maybe a sibling's bedroom: 'It was the half-eaten toast, the discarded T-shirt, the worn teddy bear peeping out from under the pillow, the sickly smell of body spray...'
* Why the dog is far too clever to be a real dog
* Things to do on a sunny day
* Fantasy bands and their song titles
* What Ellie packed in her suitcase when she ran away

Try it out and see what works for you:

2 First lines

Once upon a time...

Yes it's a cliché, but something about those words and all the stories (and Disney movies) absorbed when young can trigger a whole style of writing. Free your inner princess/wicked fairy/frog and start your story below. Or try one of these:

* The dragon came on a Saturday and refused to leave.
* A green box appeared on the doorstep.
* He never expected to like the aliens as much as he did.
* When I am 30 I shall...
* I remember when...

SOME DOS AND DON'TS

* Don't worry about spelling and grammar. Only *you* are reading it.
  And you can fix that later if you need to.
* Do set the timer on your phone for 10 minutes as a minimum.
  Keep writing for the whole time without going back and crossing out.
* Don't listen to the critic on your shoulder. Even the most famous of writers
  will have that nagging voice saying it's not good enough/you'll never finish it/
  you're not a real writer. This happens to everybody so don't worry about it and
  banish the inner critic. Be kind to yourself.
* Do look back afterwards at what you've written and pick out
  a sentence with a highlighter pen that stands out to you.
  Be proud of your writing.
* Don't expect it to be polished and marvellous at the first
  attempt. The books on your shelf will have been through
  many drafts and edits. Writing is all about the process.

More ideas to keep you writing...

Browse a newspaper or magazine. Pick a story that sparks
your interest as a starting point: a tortoise that was found
10 miles from home; a robot that can read your emotions;
a woman rescued from a mountain.

Write up a dream that you remember. If it's one that scared you,
see if you can write a different ending.

Pick three words from the dictionary. Now try to weave them
into the same story. How about:

* Earring, lock, seal.
* Assassin, gondola, pug.
* Burn, hoop, typewriter.

TIME FOR PLAN B?

You may have your life all mapped out, with dreams and hopes for the future. But things don't always go according to plan. So prepare yourself and learn to adapt if your life doesn't follow the route you'd imagined...

What are your aspirations in life? Going to university and getting a degree, or maybe securing your dream job by the age of 20 and having a family by 25? Now imagine none of this happens. How would you react? You may feel like a failure, vulnerable and unsure. You might blame yourself and struggle to picture or even consider another future because this one was so clear in your mind. The point is, sometimes life happens and your perfectly outlined plan has to change, because as hard as you may try, you aren't always in complete control of it all. This doesn't necessarily mean your unplanned life will be bad... in fact, it might even be better, although that's not always obvious at first.

So have you considered that you could still be happy even if you don't shine academically? Or imagined yourself not getting your dream job and travelling the world instead? Controlling your life may be empowering – but it can also be tiring. Unexpected challenges, on the other hand, can be a blessing in disguise: they release you from the pressure that comes with expectation, make you free to look at life with a new pair of eyes, and offer new opportunities that you may never have looked for before.

New adventures

When something unexpected comes your way, take a step back. Think about what you truly want. Could the misfortune be a sign, a door opening to something you wouldn't have considered before? Events in life can shake you to the core, but they can also stop you from living on autopilot. And once you realise that life is unpredictable and not obstacle-free (for anyone) and that dreams change with time and circumstances, it's possible to enjoy living in the present more.

Whenever you hit a brick wall, focus on what you can control and how you can make things better for yourself. Not what you wish to happen, but what you can actually do. Whatever has happened has happened, so try not to feel sorry for yourself (for long anyway) because Plan A didn't work. Instead regain some control by choosing your Plan B. So if, when the time comes, you're not accepted into your preferred university, you can still apply for apprenticeships, try alternative educational routes, or gain some work experience first to show your commitment. The key is not learning how to avoid unexpected situations (because by definition, you can't), but knowing how to react to them. At first, some life-changing events might feel too painful to face but overcoming tough times will make you more resilient in the long run. So be prepared, be brave, take up the challenge and learn something from it.

The road to recovery

Try to see life like an eventful car journey: a long road littered with bumps, obstacles and crossroads. Sometimes it might be an uncomfortable ride and occasionally you'll get lost, but if you can keep driving and work out an alternative route, you'll eventually find your way back to the main road. And remember, it's often not the speed you go at or the destination that matters, but rather the journey itself.

'NOT UNTIL WE ARE LOST DO WE BEGIN TO UNDERSTAND OURSELVES'

Henry David Thoreau

LIVE AND LEARN

So things haven't gone as expected. Take a moment to breathe and calm yourself. Now focus on how you can make changes for the better. What are your options? Grab a piece of paper and list your ideas. One of them might even turn out to be better than your original plan...

* Stay positive. It's important to have dreams, but if they don't come true, don't stall your life by imagining it's the end of the world.
* Accept the situation as it is, practise optimism and speak to friends and family so you don't struggle on your own.
* If you're dealing with a major crisis, it's natural to feel overwhelmed more easily, so set aside some time for yourself.
* Challenges are life lessons. Even if they weaken you at first, they will eventually make you stronger.
* If you ever doubt yourself, remember what you have achieved so far.
* With hindsight, you might see the good in what didn't work out, but for now, move on by focusing on what you can control.

TEEN Breathe

TEEN BREATHE is a trademark of Guild of Master Craftsman Publications Ltd

First published 2022 by Ammonite Press
an imprint of Guild of Master Craftsman Publications Ltd
Castle Place, 166 High Street, Lewes, East Sussex, BN7 1XU, United Kingdom

www.ammonitepress.com
www.teenbreathe.co.uk

Editorial: Susie Duff, Josie Fletcher, Catherine Kielthy, Jane Roe

Publisher: Jonathan Grogan
Designer: Jo Chapman

Words credits: Dawattie Basdeo, Claire Blackmore, Vicky H Bourne, Tracy Calder, Jenny Cockle, Claire Cook, Lorna Cowan, Tracy Darnton, Colin Davies, Natasha Denness, Donna Finlay, Lauren Goodchild, Anne Guillot, Nigel Huddleston, Ashley Lampard, Milla Lascelles, Hattie Nixon, Glen Richardson, Sarah Rodrigues, Carol Anne Strange, Xenia Taliotis

Illustrations: Anieszka Banks, Teresa Arroyo Corcobado, Lou Baker Smith, Agnesbic, Matt Chinworth, Jacqueline Colley, Cat Finnie, Beatrix Hatcher, Claire van Heukelom, Stephanie Hofmann, Vanessa Lovegrove, Sam Pernoski, Merle Schewe, Helma Speksnijder, Silvia Stecher, Sara Thielker, Cheryl Thuesday, Rose Wong, Shutterstock.com

Cover illustration: Charly Clements

ISBN 978 1 78145 471 8

Colour reproduction by GMC Reprographics
Printed and bound in Turkey

AMMONITE
PRESS